IMAGES
of America

OLD SWEDES CHURCH
AND HISTORIC SITE

IMAGES
of America

OLD SWEDES CHURCH
AND HISTORIC SITE

Betsy V. Christopher

ARCADIA
PUBLISHING

Published by Arcadia Publishing
Charleston, South Carolina

Printed in the United States of America

Library of Congress Control Number: 2023937943

For all general information, please contact Arcadia Publishing:
Telephone 843-853-2070
Fax 843-853-0044
E-mail sales@arcadiapublishing.com

Visit us on the Internet at www.arcadiapublishing.com

This work is dedicated to Charlie and Claire,
my partners in historic preservation.

CONTENTS

ACKNOWLEDGMENTS

Many, many thanks to the following, without whom this work would not be complete nor correct: Kathleen Abplanalp, PhD, architectural historian; Andrea L. Anderson, laboratory coordinator, Department of Anthropology, University of Delaware; Lu Ann De Cunzo, PhD, RPA, professor, Department of Anthropology, University of Delaware; Michael J. Emmons Jr., assistant director, Center for Historic Architecture & Design, Biden School of Public Policy and Administration, University of Delaware; Charlie Murphy; Brandi Bey Neal, artistic director, Christina Cultural Arts Center; Kyle Parks, assistant director of public programs and engagement at the Kalmar Nyckel Foundation; Lori Smith; Pamela Stevenson; Richard Steadham, president of the Timen Stiddem Society; and Cindy Waksmonski.

Equal thanks go to the following institutions: the Delaware Art Museum; the Episcopal Diocese of Delaware; Historical and Interpretive Collections of the Franklin Institute; the Library Company of Philadelphia; the Library of Congress; Trinity Episcopal Church, Wilmington, Delaware; Special Collections, University of Delaware Library, Museums and Press; and the Wyeth Foundation for American Art/Artists Rights Society.

The 2015 Historic Structures Report prepared by the experts of Frens & Frens LLC, restoration architects, was an invaluable source of fact and inspiration for this project. Those experts were Dale H. Frens, AIA, principal architect-in-charge; Carol J. Quigley, principal investigator; Philip Pendleton, architectural historian; Kathleen Abplanalp, image sourcing and interpretation; Richard Wolbers, historic paint analysis; John Carr, gravemarker conditions survey; and Milner and Carr Conservation LLC, gravemarker conservation survey.

Unless otherwise noted, all images are from the Archive and Collections of the Old Swedes Foundation Inc.

Please note that the names Holy Trinity and Old Swedes refer to the same church.

INTRODUCTION

For 60 years, the families of the fledgling colony of New Sweden gathered for worship in rudimentary log churches built by the Swedish and Finnish settlers. Established in 1638 when the Swedish vessels *Kalmar Nyckel* and *Fogel Grip* landed at "The Rocks," the rock outcropping that served the colonists as a natural wharf on the banks of a river flowing into the Delaware, the colony's first building was a fort. They named it and the river it overlooked for their young queen, Christina of Sweden.

Small and dimly lit, the first church within Fort Christina and its successor at Crane Hook (Tranhook) were central to the life of the New Sweden colony. Since 1688, when its pastor Lars Lock died, the congregation had lacked a priest, though ably led by the remarkable layman Charles Springer. In 1697, however, all that was about to change with the arrival of Swedish priest Erik Björk, sent to take charge of the church at Crane Hook on the west side of the Delaware River. Upon arrival, Reverend Björk was almost immediately convinced of the need for a larger, more permanent structure in a better location, and he set about to make it happen.

In less than a year, on May 28, 1698, the cornerstone of the new church was set at the juncture of its north and east walls. Reverend Björk had brokered a compromise on the location, received a donation of land from church warden John Stalcop, successfully insisted on a larger building than originally planned, and, to allay fears of excessive cost, promised to raise one-third of the construction cost himself.

The church's new location was on a slight rise, a knoll 400 yards north of the Christina River and the colony's original fort, where there had been a burying ground since 1638. John Stalcop's donation, about three acres of sufficiently high ground adjacent to the known graves, was enough for the church building and walkways on the south and west sides.

A true community effort, it is recorded that 81 people gave the equivalent of 932 days' work. Equally important were the contributions of those who housed and fed the work crews, secured building materials, and raised funds for the construction itself. Helga Trefaldighet Kyrka (Holy Trinity Church) was consecrated on Trinity Sunday, June 4, 1699. Remarkably, the building was completed in a little over a year, "in so wild a country in so short a time, and above all my expectations and against so many oppositions," wrote Reverend Björk. The existence of Holy Trinity is, in fact, a tribute to his unflagging energy and creative vision. He negotiated contracts with the carpenters, masons, joiners, and other artisans, superintended the construction, and raised the necessary funds for its completion.

History surrounds you as you walk through the burial ground to Old Swedes Church. The first of the eight churches of New Sweden, Holy Trinity (Old Swedes) Church is recognized as one of the oldest extant churches in America in regular use as a house of worship. One of the best surviving remnants of the New Sweden colony, the church building is remarkably little changed since its construction was completed.

While the New Sweden colony was short-lived (1638–1655), its settlers had a profound and enduring impact in the region, with settlements along the Delaware River in what is now Delaware, New Jersey, and Pennsylvania. Place names reflect the Swedish heritage: Christiana, Delaware; Swedesboro, New Jersey; Upland, Pennsylvania; Swedesford Road in Chester and Montgomery Counties in Pennsylvania. When Philadelphia City Hall was built (1872–1901), sculptor Alexander Milne Calder placed four colossal bronze statues on the four corners of the cupola below William Penn: a Native American man and woman and a Swedish man and woman, each holding a child. The City of Philadelphia's flag colors of blue and yellow commemorate the original Swedish colonization of the Philadelphia area. Likewise, the city flag of Wilmington, Delaware, is the Swedish flag, stamped with the city seal.

Swedes and Finns also introduced the log house method of construction to the New World. Tall, straight tree trunks laid horizontally atop each other were secured with interlocking corners made by notching the logs at the ends. Requiring only simple tools, a log house could be built in a short time. One of the oldest log houses in the United States, whose address is appropriately Swedesboro Road in New Jersey, was built around 1638–1643.

Certainly, the short-lived colony generated among Swedes a strong and lasting interest in America. Every year, Old Swedes Historic Site, which includes Holy Trinity, the burial ground, and the Hendrickson House, welcomes visitors from Sweden and Finland and visitors of Swedish and Finnish descent from across the United States. The Wilmington region has benefited from the city's participation in the Sister Cities program, annually welcoming students from Kalmar, Sweden. Members of the Swedish royal family make regular visits to Wilmington, and to Old Swedes in particular, to commemorate significant anniversaries. Most recently, Holy Trinity welcomed King Carl XVI Gustaf and Queen Silvia in 2013 in celebration of the 375th anniversary of the Swedes' landing at The Rocks.

The burial ground surrounding Holy Trinity predates the church by 60 years, established at the time Fort Christina was built. Soon after the church was built, the congregation contributed posts, palings, and nails for a wooden fence to enclose the churchyard. Burials were initially limited to members of the congregation, and families were simply buried next to one another, creating family plots. In the mid-1800s, however, the western portion of the graveyard was laid out in lots with a driveway and paths, and the lots were sold to any who wished to buy. By then, the wood fence had been replaced with a more substantial stone wall, and some family plots were enclosed by decorative iron fencing. Today, the burial ground holds more than 1,200 grave markers and is the final resting place of an estimated 15,000 people.

In 2024, Holy Trinity will celebrate its 325th year, having endured as Wilmington grew up around it. While the simply designed yet substantial church has remained remarkably intact, its surroundings have evolved through the decades. The early Swedish settlers established farms, mills, and stone quarries to the north and east, while heavy industry such as shipbuilding, railcar manufacturing, and steam engines grew up along the Christina River to the south in the 19th century. Modest housing for workers employed in those industries was densely built to the west and north of the church property.

The buildings, the land, and the history they embody are a treasure to be carefully preserved; their importance is such that the church was declared a national historic landmark in the early 1960s, and the church and burial ground were added as a unit of First State National Historical Park, Delaware's first national park, created in 2015. The church's archives hold a wealth of information for those of Swedish heritage. Of equal importance is the community of faith that has been sustained for so many years by the leadership of its ministers and the loyalty of its congregation. As the iron letters driven into the west wall of the new church proclaim, "If God be for us, who can be against us?"

One

THE COLONY OF NEW SWEDEN

The church at Tranhook (Crane Hook), built in 1667 on the south side of the Christina River, succeeded the first church of the New Sweden colony, constructed within the walls of Fort Christina. Built of logs in a blockhouse style, this church's projecting second story served as a defensive structure against external threats. Worshipers were primarily Swedes and Finns but also included people of English, Dutch, and German origin.

— *Drawing by Walter Stewart from description of Reverend Erik Björk*

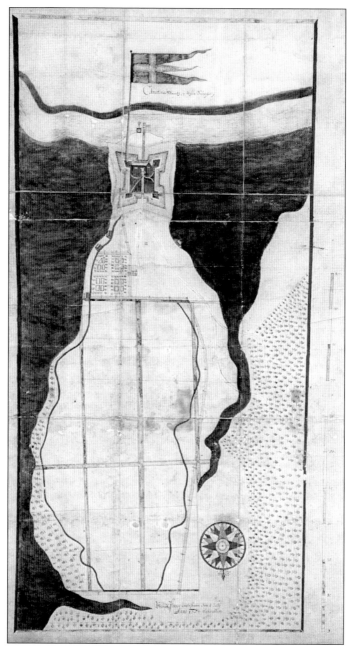

Drawn on-site by Swedish engineer/mapmaker Peter Lindstrom, this 1654 map shows Fort Christina and is the earliest known depiction of the foundation of the New Sweden colony. The fort named for Queen Christina of Sweden was located at the confluence of the Brandywine and Christina Rivers, about two miles upstream from the mouth of the Christina on the Delaware River. Led by Peter Minuit, the Swedish ships *Kalmar Nyckel* and *Fogel Grip* landed here at The Rocks, an outcropping that served as a natural wharf, in 1638. The site was considered easily defensible as well as a prime location for trade with the local Lenni Lenape. In Lindstrom's detailed drawing, the first log cabins in America are visible—the soldiers' barracks and the storehouse for the safekeeping of furs and trade goods. (The Timen Stiddem Society.)

Excavations at five sites around the foundation of Old Swedes Church were conducted in 2015 by University of Delaware students learning archaeological field methods. The south porch unit, a yard in front of the original church entrance, was chosen to see what kinds of activities were represented outside the church's "front" door. Clothing pins, which fastened dresses and shawls, and fragments of clay smoking pipes were found, evidence of people socializing outside the church. A Native American presence at the site, evident in all excavations, was indicated by a predominance of lithic (stone) material, such as quartz and fine-grained chert. There are flakes discarded from stone tool manufacturing and flakes modified to be stone tools. The relatively few historic artifacts may be a result of previous eras' construction projects (Both, Department of Anthropology, University of Delaware.)

The external stairs leading to the second-floor gallery (to students' left, out of sight) were added in 1774. It is presumed that the original stairs had the same form and general appearance of the exterior stairs today, but there exists no physical evidence. Students discovered a mottled level similar to that in the excavation at the western third of the North Profile wall. At first, the mixture of yellow and dark brown soils looked very similar to the grave shafts at the North and South Buttress units, but ground penetrating radar surveys did not identify any shafts oriented north-south. Further investigation revealed a post hole/mold of approximately 10 inches (pictured above) about a yard away from the existing double-door entrance, just off center. The current interpretation places the large post as part of an earlier external stairway construction, perhaps the original 1774 construction. (Both, Department of Anthropology, University of Delaware.)

Swedes and Finns brought the log cabin to North America; the earliest extant example, in New Jersey, dates to 1638. With few tools, one could be built in a matter of days. This example, the 19th-century Johan Stalcop/Thomas Bird house, is an 18-by-20-foot structure made of oak logs hewn on the front and back sides to create flat walls. (Library of Congress, Prints & Photographs Division, HABS DE-131, 2-PRICO, 2-2.)

Delaware schoolchildren in the 1980s enjoyed exploring the Stalcop/Bird log cabin, then in Fort Christina State Park, one block from Old Swedes Historic Site. Preserved by the Fenimore family, it was originally located at Prices Corner, west of Wilmington. Threatened by the expansion of Route 141 and construction of a gas station, the structure was moved in 1962. Neglected, it was destroyed by fire and vandalism in the early 1990s. (Photograph by Pam Stevenson.)

This photograph from the June 1963 edition of the *American-Swedish News Exchange* is captioned: "Seated between Jasper Hill, the Big White Owl of Youngs Harbor, Ont., Willard Thomas of Anadarko, Oklahoma, and Cephas W. Snake of Bothwell, Ont. is Olle Norbeck, Swedish expert on American Indians. He traced the Delaware Indians across the U.S. to Oklahoma and Canada when the Swedish Government wanted to fulfill a 325-year-old promise to the tribe which once settled on the banks of the Delaware River." The colonial governor of New Sweden had invited representatives to come to Sweden but because the hazards of ocean travel in the 17th century could not promise a safe return; the invitation remained standing and was finally accepted in 1963. The visitors are shown in the courtyard of the medieval Kalmar Castle in southeast Sweden. The first Swedish ships to sail to the New World embarked from Kalmar.

A granite marker was erected by the Historical Society of Delaware in 1896 for the 200th anniversary of Crane Hook Church. The church was built close to the Delaware and Christina Rivers for the convenience of its widespread congregation, many of whom traveled by water. The original location eventually became the property of the Port of Delaware, which restricted public access. The monument was relocated in 2013 to the Old Swedes churchyard.

Two

REV. ERIK BJÖRK AND THE BUILDING OF HOLY TRINITY

To the 17th century Swedish community, this was Helga Trefaldighet Kyrka. To later English speakers and today, it is Holy Trinity Church. This image depicts the church as it likely appeared in 1699, after the initial construction was completed. It is one in a series of three scenes in a lithograph dated 1938 by Wilmington artist David Reyam (1864–1943). The images illustrate the development of the building: early 1699, in 1798 after the south porch was added, and in its present form, with the 1803 addition of the bell tower and cupola.

Rev. Erik Tobias Björk (1668–1740), a Lutheran missionary sent by Sweden, arrived in the colony of New Sweden in 1697. He first served the congregation of Tranhook (Crane Hook), a small wooden church two miles from Fort Christina. Shortly after his first sermon on July 11, 1697, he began advocating for a new, larger church to be built north of the Christina River. Under his leadership, funds were raised; contributions of land, lumber, sand, and stone were made by members of the congregation; artisans were hired; and the building, begun in 1698, was completed in just over a year. This portrait by an unknown Swedish artist depicts Björk age 60 when he had returned to Sweden to oversee the three congregations of Falun parish. Old Swedes' painting is a copy of the 1728 original, presented to the church in 1899 by the Falun copper mining company to mark Holy Trinity's 200th anniversary. The original hangs in Kristine Church in Falun, Sweden.

Know all men by these presents that I John Stalcop doe acknowledge that I have fully received of the Rev. Minister Mr. ... & Charles Springer, by two bills & obligations bearing date the 9 of June 1696. one wch: I was indebted to John hance Steelm... of fifty pounds in silver money, and the other I was indebted unto my brother Pietter Stalcop, wch. bills they have took of the sd. persons, and now I have recd. them of the sd. Minister & Charles Springer, which bills is in all one hundred pounds, wch: is in part for the land wch. I have sould unto Christeen congregation for the use of a Minister whereunto I have sett my hand & seale the 29 Sept. 1699.

Longtime congregants first at Crane Hook Church and then at Holy Trinity, the Stalcop family owned hundreds of acres of land in the area. Church warden John (Johan) Stalcop (b. 1662) gave to the congregation a small piece of land, about three acres, on which to build its new church. It was not until 1722, however, that Stalcop's sons Israel and Jonas formally deeded the land to the Holy Trinity congregation. The original document is in the Old Swedes Foundation archives. A measure of the Stalcop real estate holdings can be estimated by an agreement in 1699 wherein Johan Stalcop agreed to sell two parcels of land to the congregation, totaling about 500 acres. One of those parcels, of 228 acres, was to the north of the churchyard comprising what is now central Wilmington, according to the deed recorded on May 18, 1703.

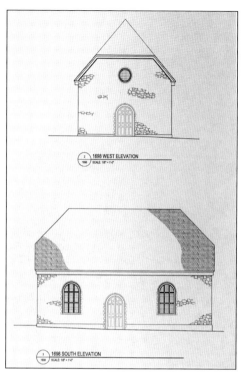

This elevation shows Holy Trinity Church as originally built. Measuring 66 feet by 36 feet with walls 20 feet high, it was designed as an "auditory" church—a unified large space with no partition between the chancel and the nave. Largely an invention of English architect Christopher Wren, the design is a physical manifestation of the Reformation, allowing worshipers to both see and hear what was occurring at the altar.

While this floor plan drawn in 1934 for the Historic American Buildings Survey (HABS) shows the additions to Holy Trinity made throughout its history, the original floor plan of a wide central aisle and two narrower cross aisles running north-south in a space twice as long as it was wide is evident. The primary contractor was Joseph Yard, a Philadelphia mason and bricklayer. (Library of Congress, Prints & Photographs Division, HABS DEL, 2-WILM, 1-7.)

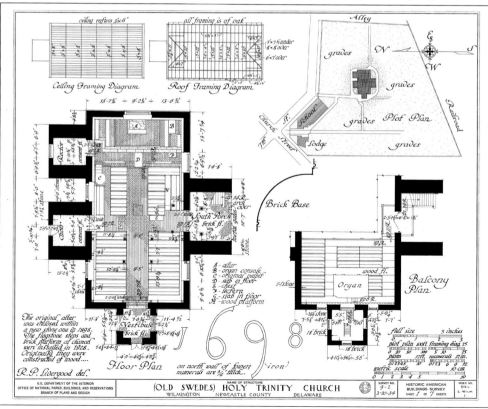

This 19th-century reproduction of a pen-and-India-ink drawing by Ethan Comly shows the church from the southwest and is entitled "The Swedes Church, Wilmington, Del. 1698." Comly's original image dates to after 1774 when the gallery stairs shown in the south porch were built and prior to 1803 when the brick bell tower and wooden belfry were added to the west end of the church, seen at left.

In this 1934 HABS photograph, characteristic Swedish church architecture features can be seen. Old Swedes Church is a plain yet substantial stone rectangular structure with a wood-shingled, jerkinhead (hipped) roof. Much of the stone, Delaware blue granite, came from parishioner Ashmund Stidham's land north of the church. The mortar sparkles with bits of ground oyster shell. (Library of Congress, Prints & Photographs Division, HABS DEL, 2-WILM, 1-15.)

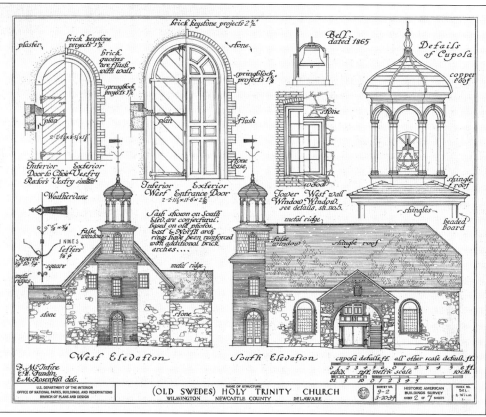

The Historic American Buildings Survey, the nation's first federal preservation program, began in 1933 to document America's architectural heritage, from monuments and mansions to the utilitarian and vernacular. HABS came to Old Swedes in 1934 and created eight sheets of measured drawings and eight large-format photographs of the church, leaving a valuable, detailed record. (Library of Congress, Prints & Photographs Division, HABS DEL, 2-WILM, 2-7.)

At night, the date 1698 shows clearly on the brick bell tower of the church, marking the year construction began. Wrought iron numerals and letters can still be seen on the north, south, and east walls, forged by blacksmith Mathias De Foss, a congregant of the church. The numbers and letters told in abbreviated Latin words and phrases when and by whom the church was built.

A collection of iron letters is preserved in the foundation archives. The west end letters were found intact behind the western portico in 1899, and some were placed on the north wall of the tower. The inscriptions high up on the exterior walls of the church were originally painted in red lead and on one side acknowledged Pennsylvania proprietor William Penn, English king William III, Swedish king Charles XI, and Pastor Erik Björk.

IN MEMORY OF

CHARLES (CARL CHRISTOPHER) SPRINGER

BORN STOCKHOLM SWEDEN 1658
CAME TO AMERICA 1678
DIED WILMINGTON, DELAWARE 1738

A FOUNDER AND BUILDER OF THIS CHURCH. WARDEN,
VESTRYMAN, AND COUNCILLOR FROM THE FOUNDING
UNTIL HIS DEATH. HIS BODY RESTS BENEATH THIS
EAST WALL OF THE SOUTH PORTICO

Charles (Carl Christopherson) Springer (1658–1738) is, along with Rev. Erik Björk, perhaps the most significant figure in the early history of Old Swedes. A well-educated man who spoke five languages, he survived kidnapping, indentured servitude, and a 400-mile journey to Delaware to become a leader of the New Sweden colony. It was primarily due to his efforts that new ministers and books were sent to the colony in 1697; in their absence, as the most literate of the congregation, Springer conducted services and wrote out wills, deeds, and other legal documents in English. He assisted Björk in overseeing fundraising for and construction of Holy Trinity, and for years after, served the church as warden, vestryman, and councilor. The father of 11 children, he farmed two plantations and was appointed a justice of the New Castle County courts. He was buried close to the south wall of the church. In 1762, when the south porch was added to buttress the failing south wall, it was decided not to remove his remains, and so today his grave lies within Old Swedes.

This early painting, an oil on wood board, shows the southeast corner of the church, south porch, and bell tower. The artist is unidentified, but the painting can be dated to the mid-19th century. The south porch was added in 1760 to buttress the south wall of the church; like the north wall, it had begun to bow outwards due to a number of factors: the weight of the roof, inadequate roof framing for the vaulted ceiling, and a relatively shallow foundation. The bell tower was finished in 1803. The church in this painting resembles the building seen in the painting by Frederick deBourg Richards around 1843. Both show the windows shuttered and thus may have been painted prior to the 1842 renovation. A label on the reverse notes that the painting was presented to Old Swedes by "Chas. L. Reese, Jr. Warden, 1928."

No images of the church in its first century are known to exist. However, there is an imaginary representation of Old Swedes' earliest days in this watercolor by Wilmington artist Bayard Taylor Berndt (1908–1987). Berndt was a student of Frank Schoonover and N.C. Wyeth; his work is historically accurate as well as nostalgic. Celebrated for his paintings of regional landscapes and local scenes in historic context, Berndt used this image for a family Christmas card. The church's porches, open-arched bell tower, and close proximity to the Christina River are all clearly illustrated. Several sailing ships are moored on the north bank of the river, and parishioners are arriving by foot, sled, and sleigh through the snow. What is also apparent is that in its early years, unlike today, the church stood out as the largest, tallest building in the area, its solid bulk conveying its importance to the community.

Three

THE 18TH AND 19TH CENTURIES

Holy Trinity's bell tower and welcoming, open door are seen from Seventh Street in this photograph dating to the 1960s. The bronze plaque on the left-hand column offers the name of the church in Swedish (Helga Trefaldighet Kyrka) and gives a concise history of its origins. Another plaque, this one designating the church as a national historic landmark, can be spotted to the right of the bell tower door.

An 1845 drawing of the church by Benjamin Ferris of Wilmington is pictured here. The engraving is one of the few illustrations in Elizabeth Montgomery's memoir *Reminiscences of Wilmington in Familiar Village Tales, Ancient and New* (1851), a valuable source of information about daily Wilmington life in the first half of the 19th century, describing everything from factories, flour, and paper mills to skating parties and picnics and the replacement of the city's wooden water mains with cast iron pipes. A Wilmington native, Elizabeth (1778–1863) was the daughter of Revolutionary War hero Capt. Hugh Montgomery. Prominent in society, she taught sewing and drawing and cofounded the Female Bible Society of Wilmington. After the church was closed in 1830, she was one of a group of churchwomen who worked tirelessly to raise enough money to repair and restore the building. Elizabeth Montgomery is buried in the Old Swedes burial ground.

When the newly built Trinity Chapel opened in 1830 on the northeast corner of Fifth and King Streets, regular services at Old Swedes were discontinued, and the church was left vacant and unprotected. Already in a dilapidated state due to lack of maintenance, it suffered the ravages of weather, curious visitors, and vandalism until "the roof became leaky, the pews became broken and blackened, the pulpit was mutilated, the cushions of the chancel torn away, the windows were broken, the plastering began to fall off, and the whole interior presented a repulsive and melancholy sight," according to Rev. J.W. McCullough, pastor of Trinity Chapel. Artist R.A. Matlack documented the state of the church and churchyard in this watercolor/ink wash dated 1842 and entitled *Old Church at Wilmington*. The abandoned old Swedish church was even threatened with demolition, but a number of female parishioners rallied to raise enough money for some repairs in the mid-1830s, including re-roofing one side of the church, securing windows, and building a stone wall around the churchyard.

OLD SWEDES CHURCH

WILMINGTON, DEL.

Erected 1698

A label on the reverse of this oil painting reads, "Old Swedes Church/Erected 1698 Wilmington, De/Painted by F. DeB. Richards/1843 presented to my friend Isaiah Price Dec. 25, 1900." The newly completed renovations of 1842 no doubt sparked a renewal of interest in the church, which led Richards to paint this view not long after its reopening. The painting also illustrates the 19th-century rural cemetery movement, where cemeteries served as landscaped, parklike areas of recreation and contemplation in the midst of a crowded urban environment. A major rehabilitation of the church took place between 1840 and 1842, thanks to a significant bequest by congregant Henrietta M. Allmond, who was also a leader in the ambitious undertaking. Among the substantial changes made were the relocation of the gallery stairs from the south porch to the interior and the removal of the original box pews, many of which were damaged and were replaced with plain wooden benches. A raised wooden platform was installed over the brick floor, eliminating the need to step down into the church from the western entrance.

This is one of the earliest photographs of the church building. The bell tower (1803) has been added. It was the hope of church leaders that constructing the tower to make Holy Trinity the tallest building in Wilmington would increase its prominence and attract new worshipers to its congregation. The three-part structure on the west wall consisted of a brick base, wood-framed middle section, and a cupola. In this image, the ground floor arches are still open as originally built, affording ventilation to the congregation. They were filled in with heavy, windowed doors later in the century. The porches on either side of the building are clearly seen; they were added to buttress the walls of the church, which were bowing under the weight of the barrel-vaulted roof. Their addition created porticos around the doors on the north and south walls. Buildings of the McCullough Iron Works can be seen in the background on the right, with workers' brick rowhouses in the left background.

This photograph showing the ivy-covered south porch of Old Swedes can be dated to before 1892 through several clues. Though there is a second-floor door to the gallery visible, there are no exterior stairs. A previous renovation (1840–1842) had moved the stairs to inside the church, likely to encourage the use of the south porch as the main entrance and possibly to prevent vandalism. The gallery stairs were relocated from inside the church in the renovations of 1899, which also saw iron gates installed across the south portico. Secondly, the Millikin stained glass window is not yet installed; it would replace the multipaned window on the southeast side, seen here at left, in 1892. The stained glass window honoring James A. and Anne Bayard at right was installed in 1891. The stovepipe exiting the roof at the ridgeline was removed in 1899.

The north porches were added in 1740 to brace the north wall, which had begun to bow outward due to the roof's weight and design. Concerns about the stability of the masonry wall were raised as early as 1733. Essentially roofed buttresses, the porches were built with four-and-a-half-foot-thick solid stone walls—more than twice the width of the sanctuary walls—extending more than 13 feet.

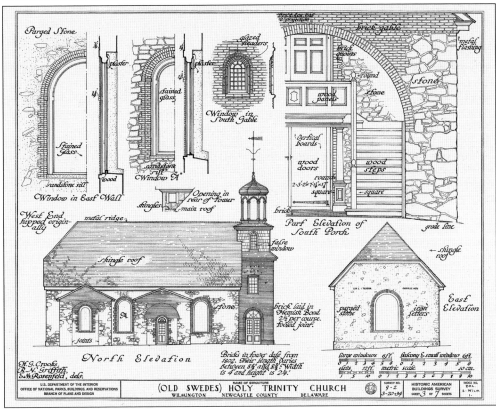

The new porches were placed at the existing entrance doors; to provide maximum support, they overlapped the two north windows. Those windows are thus smaller than the south windows. The porches were left open until the early 19th century, when the northeast porch's doorway (at left in north elevation) was boarded up to create the sacristy, according to 1847 church records. (Library of Congress, Prints & Photographs Division, HABS DEL, 2-WILM, 3-17.)

In this image by an unidentified photographer taken some time prior to 1880, the north elevation of the church is seen, revealing the open arched doors of the ivy-covered bell tower. The quaint, small-paned sash windows, which are presumed to date to the 1842 restoration, have not yet been replaced by memorial stained glass windows, whose installation began in the late 19th century. Some years earlier, an arched window was installed in the northeast porch and an arched door in the northwest. The windows feature wooden board-and-batten shutters, which matched the plain, similarly constructed door that opens to a vestibule giving access to the interior. Shutters were added in the restoration of 1842 as a protective measure since the church's windows suffered greatly during its period of abandonment (1830–1836). The arched fanlight window sections were covered with fixed panels, and the shutters below constructed as rectangular panels, perhaps easier and less expensive to build.

In this 1874 bird's-eye view of Wilmington's East Side, the proximity of Old Swedes Church (upper center) to the Christina River can clearly be seen. The Gothic Revival arch built in 1847 as the main entrance to the churchyard sits at the corner of Church and Seventh Streets. Its roof and tall spires were the height of a two-story building and its design was in step with the Gothic style then popular in church architecture. The Philadelphia, Wilmington & Baltimore (PW&B) Railroad cuts a diagonal across the map; the PW&B purchased a strip of land along the eastern edge of the burial ground in 1837. Heavy industry is well developed along the river, including Pusey and Jones shipbuilders (1853); the Lobdell Car Wheel Company (1831); Jackson & Sharp, manufacturers of railcars and ships (1863); the McCullough Iron Company (1865) and the Diamond State Iron Company (1853). (H.H. Bailey, "Wilmington, Delaware," 1874. Library of Congress Geography and Map Division, Washington, DC.)

This photograph from a glass negative was taken by Marriott Canby Morris. Morris's relatives, including grandparents Merrit Canby and Eliza (Tatnall) Canby and aunt Anna (Tatnall) Canby, lived in Wilmington. Morris (1863–1948) was an amateur Philadelphia photographer who photographed many Wilmington landscapes as well as his relatives' residences. A member of a prominent Quaker family descended from Philadelphia merchant Anthony Morris, Marriott was also a philanthropist, executor and trustee of estates, founder of the Germantown Boys' Club, and an avid bicyclist on the high wheel or penny farthing bicycle. This photograph is marked "Taken from Sixth Street" and dated December 26, 1883. Morris also notes that the day was sunny. He kept detailed notes of his photographic activities in pocket-sized notebooks, recording camera settings, the date and time he took the photograph, and even comments on the quality of his images. (The Library Company of Philadelphia.)

The south porch was added to the south wall in 1762 as another measure to stabilize the church walls, much as the two porches were added more than 20 years previously to the north wall. An expanding congregation led to the 1774 construction of a second-floor gallery over the back third of the sanctuary, holding 25 pews. The stairs to the second-floor gallery, seen at right inside the porch, were also added in 1774. The only access to the second floor, the staircase was built outside the church to preserve seating space on the first floor. This photograph shows the staircase as it looked after the 1899 restoration, when it was moved from inside the church to its original location. Note that the doors were painted white, thus covering decades of historical graffiti. Both sets of doors are original to the gallery's construction. The second-floor doors are bifold doors, hinged in the middle and latched on the left.

Imagine the surprise of discovering graffiti dating to the 1700s covering the south-side doors when more than 30 layers of paint were removed in preparation for the 300th anniversary. Initials, names, dates, and drawings of houses, hearts, a ship, and even Old Swedes Church itself can be found, with 1711 the oldest legible date. Historian Michael Emmons estimates that 150 of the carvings contain a date, with most between 1825 and 1842. "The church was essentially abandoned for a period during most of the 1830s . . . with an uncertain future—and at the mercy of loiterers carrying penknives," he writes, adding, "It's unsurprising that this broadside, likely dating to the 1830s, was once posted around the grounds of the churchyard at Holy Trinity. It declared that 'All persons are prohibited, under a penalty of FIVE DOLLARS, . . . [from] breaking the trees, shrubbery or flowers—walking, sitting, or lying upon the graves or monuments—defacing the church, or tombs, by marking or cutting, with knife, pencil, or otherwise.' "

The two sets of double doors are almost completely covered with graffiti. It is not surprising to find a concentration of graffiti during this time, though, since the early part of the 19th century saw "a very strong culture of marking public spaces," according to historian Michael Emmons. Not only the doors, but the pulpit, pews, and even grave markers suffered vandalism when the church was left abandoned.

Several of the inscribed names are those of families long associated with Old Swedes, suggesting that adding one's name to the church doors may have been an honor granted those who gave a gift or service to the church or in commemoration of a wedding, anniversary, or death. Some full names and place names and the obvious care taken with others indicate that not all the carving was done surreptitiously.

The wooden doors of Old Swedes were not the only canvas for graffiti artists. Carvings in stone can be found at various heights on every exterior wall, some likely dating to the building's construction in 1698–1699, as builders were known to "sign" their work. Set into the west wall of the south porch is a date stone marking its completion in 1762 and identifying its builder, mason Cornelius Hines.

The date 1817 occurs twice on this stone along with a variety of initials, such as "EV" and "GNI," and what may be a full name, "ID I(J)ones." Some of the carving in these stones is very fine and must have taken time. Though weathered, many of the inscriptions can be seen high above ground level, made by builders on ladders or scaffolding.

The four walls originally featured iron letters and numbers forged by blacksmith Matthias de Foss. Abbreviated Latin letters on the west wall asked, "If God be for us, who can be against us?" The east wall letters proclaimed, in Latin, *LUX-L.I. TENEBR ORIENS-EX ALTO* or "Light from on high shines in the darkness." Over the years, some letters have fallen off or been taken as relics.

Congregant Thomas Cole, a native of Ireland, supervised the design and construction of a bell tower on the west end of the church in 1803. Open on three sides, the three-stage tower acted as a new entrance and vestibule to the main church structure. Cole added his name to the tower's south side—"TS Cole"—and is buried with his wife a few yards away from his work.

Choir members gather outside the church in the late 1800s. From left to right are (first row) Mrs. M. Baxter, choirmother; Linda E. Cassetian; Annie Orr; Marion Quinn; Bessie Birnie; Emma Sermes; Lillie Greene; Gertrude Greene; Blanche Ziegrist; Sarah Mason; Elsie Mason; Rev. Chas. Clask; and Rev. Frederick M. Kirkus, rector; (second row) Charles Ingham; Sydney Greene; Walter Heal; Frank Heal; Ivy Sermes; Leroy Sawin; William Cochran; Maria Churchman; Ada Marden; Reverend Judge, and Rev. Albert C. Clay, vicar.

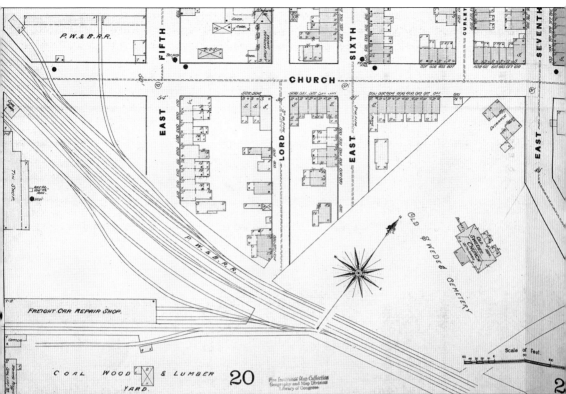

This Sanborn fire insurance map dated 1884 shows Old Swedes and its burial ground (at right) surrounded by industry and densely built working-class housing. The Philadelphia, Wilmington & Baltimore Railroad tracks cut diagonally across between Old Swedes and the railroad's freight car repair shop, tin shop, and a coal, wood, and lumberyard to the south and east. Trinity Parish had sold a strip of land from the burial ground to the newly established railroad in 1837 to raise money. Nearby is a slaughterhouse and a vacant "Morocco" factory, or leather tannery. The main entrance to the churchyard is also shown, comprising the Gothic Revival arch and the buildings later added to it. (Library of Congress, Geography and Map Division, Sanborn Maps Collection.)

Trinity Chapel at Fifth and King Streets was built in 1829 by the parish in Wilmington's newest, more fashionable residential area. Old Swedes was by then considered too far from the center of town and in need of repairs. The new chapel held four times as many people as its predecessor. Its spire and porch were added in 1850. The building was sold in 1882. (Trinity Episcopal Church.)

The second chapel to house the congregation of Holy Trinity was built farther west in 1881, near the corner of Delaware Avenue and Adams Street. The congregation worshiped here until Trinity Episcopal Church, designed by architect Theophilus P. Chandler, was completed in 1890. This chapel became the parish house for Trinity Episcopal, which, like its predecessor Old Swedes, is listed in the National Register of Historic Places. (Trinity Episcopal Church.)

Gathered outside Old Swedes in their Sunday finery are members of the congregation. From left to right are (first row) John Quinn, Leonard Glatt, and Austin Brooks; (second row) Joe Glatt, Annie Glatt, Marion Quinn, O. Brooks, M. Baxter, Blanche McKowan, and John Brooks. This photograph is one of many donated to the Old Swedes Foundation's archives by John Quinn.

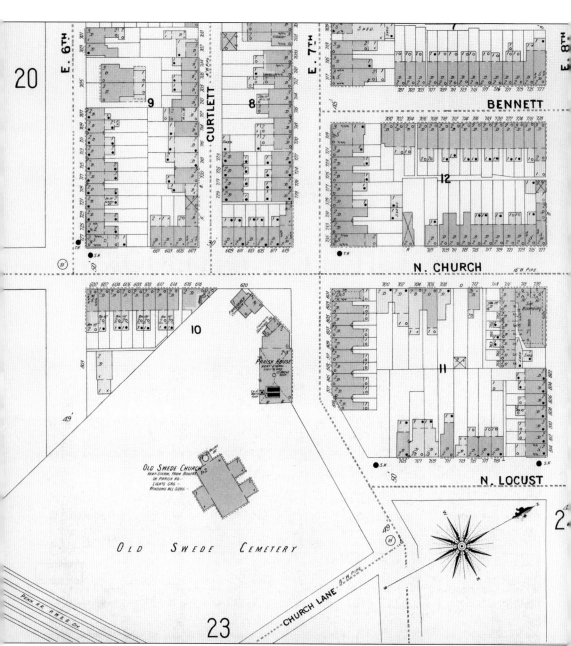

Seventeen years after the 1884 Sanborn fire insurance map on page 41, this 1901 map reveals that dense housing continued to be built around the church grounds. The map notes that the church was lit by gas and heated by steam from parish house boilers. The parish house itself, built in 1887, is marked, attached to the sexton's house and connected by the Gothic arch to the parsonage. The triangular piece of land on Church Street to the east would later be acquired by the parish and turned into public open space, and in 1948, the site of the Hendrickson House. (Library of Congress, Geography and Map Division, Sanborn Maps Collection.)

Four

THE CHURCH INTERIOR

The church is packed for a wedding in the 1950s. In the early years, people of all faiths were welcome, and the Swedish Lutheran priests traveled to other congregations that lacked a minister, going as far as Philadelphia and Lancaster, Pennsylvania, and Maryland. Church records show that many of the early baptisms, marriages, and burials were performed for families who were not members of the congregation.

Pictured is the sanctuary interior as seen prior to the 1899 renovation. The original box pews have been replaced by very plain freestanding wood benches. A wood floor completely covers the original brick floor, and the interior gallery stairs can be seen on the right; all of these elements date to the significant renovations made in 1842. The pulpit was moved to the east wall above the altar in 1793 so that congregants in the gallery could better see the priest. The gallery's slope as constructed in 1774 was not steep enough to allow a good sight line from every second-floor pew. By this time, gas light fixtures had been installed and the top of the walls decorated by a stenciled frieze. The shape of the sanctuary's barrel-vaulted ceiling can clearly be seen; it has been described as "a vessel hull turned upside down."

The walnut pulpit has been moved several times throughout the church's history. Seemingly octagonal, it is in fact made up of seven panels, capped by a moulded top rail. Only the back panel (now attached to the church's side wall) reveals the pulpit's original height, as the front panels and door panel appear to have been cut down. At first placed on the north wall close to the east end, it was moved in 1793 to sit on a base atop the altar on the east wall of the chancel. It was painted white and moved again in 1882 to the north end of the altar, against the east wall, supported by a square wooden platform. In the renovations of 1899, the paint was removed and the pulpit itself returned to its original location on the north wall. The stone baptismal font in this image, at left in front of the pulpit, is the same one now used at Trinity Episcopal Church.

The central section of herringbone bricks in the great aisle was not only the location of a warming stove for the congregation, but the bricks were taken up at Christmastime by the caretaker, who annually placed a traditional winter or Christmas tree in the cavity. In its earliest days, the church was unheated. Parishioners carried hot bricks or foot ovens to their pews. Church records for 1770 note that money was raised to purchase a stove, installed at the end of November that year. The floor's readily removable bricks, original to the 1699 church, made possible burials within the church, considered a high honor. There are 11 individuals buried under the floor, including two early pastors, Rev. Peter Tranberg (d. 1748) and Rev. Andrew Borrell (d. 1768), and the infant son of Reverend Björk (Peter, d. 1710) and the infant son of Rev. Lawrence Girelius (Peter, d. 1786).

The portraits of three consequential figures in the history of Holy Trinity were hung for years from the gallery railing. From left to right are Rev. Israel Acrelius, Rev. Erik Björk, and Rev. Peter Tranberg. Björk, the first minister, led the congregation to build the church. In 1714, he returned to Sweden to serve as pastor of the large Kopparberg Church at Falun. Tranberg came to Holy Trinity in 1742 after serving two Swedish Lutheran churches in New Jersey. Fluent in English, he worked to better include Wilmington's growing Anglican community, offering services in both Swedish and English—many Anglicans attended Old Swedes (then a Swedish Lutheran congregation) since Wilmington lacked an Anglican church. When he died in 1748, Tranberg was interred in the floor of Old Swedes. Acrelius arrived in 1749 to find a church in need of repairs, services poorly conducted, and the Swedish language "very much fallen out of use." He worked energetically for the seven years of his tenure to address those issues.

The most comprehensive restoration of the church—both interior and exterior—took place in 1899 in time for its 200th anniversary. The work was directed by Colonial Revival architect William H. Mercereau of New York and included returning the gallery staircase to the south porch, replacing the wooden benches with pew boxes of original design, returning the floor to its original level and material (brick), and adding a brick platform one brick higher than the rest of the floor between the chancel railing and front of the new pew boxes. Storm doors were installed, enclosing the bell tower portico, rotted wood in the belfry was replaced, the wood shingle roof and wood shingle bell tower finish were replaced, and the interior walls and vault were replastered and painted. Near the center of the image above is the original baptismal font, which is now in the Trinity Episcopal Church chapel on Adams Street, as seen at left.

The original altar was made of stone, five feet wide, and set against the east wall under the chancel window, surrounded by a turned walnut railing. It was hollow, covered with plaster, and painted white, as were the interior walls. Wood paneling and a marble top were likely added in 1882 when the pulpit was moved to its original location on the north wall. The altar pictured here is the redesigned version that was installed in the renovations of 1899. When the wood paneling was removed, the first altar was discovered intact. Two different sets of marks revealed the steps that led to the pulpit when it sat atop the altar and the outlines of the pulpit's base on the top. The altar's wood paneling was replaced with marble and its south-facing side was inscribed with the names of the 10 Swedish pastors who served the church in its early years. Funds for the memorial marble altar were raised by Rev. Martin B. Dunlap, vicar of the church, and the members of the young women's Bible class.

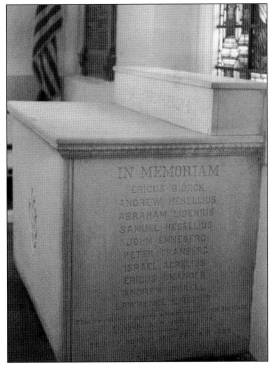

This late-19th-century photograph of the church interior shows the restored original brick floor and the section of herringbone bricks in the great aisle, which measures eight feet wide. At right behind the altar is the first organ, later replaced by a larger one (913 pipes) and relocated to the second-story gallery. Also seen are the box pews, exact replicas (made in 1899) of the original pews made of local pine in 1699, and the black walnut pulpit (left), restored to its original finish. The pulpit is believed to be original to the church's construction; in church records noting the contributions of the congregation—labor, materials, and money—the names of those who donated walnut for the pulpit are specifically listed and can be seen at the pulpit today. Much of the 1899 restoration, including the replica pews, was funded by the Colonial Dames of America's Delaware, Pennsylvania, Maryland, and New York chapters.

The antique brass lectern, adorned by an eagle, was presented to Holy Trinity in 1902 by Helen Rogers Bradford of Wilmington. Bradford gave the lectern and an Oxford edition Bible to the church in memory of her son Thomas Budd Bradford, who died aged 10 in 1900. Eagle lecterns have been commonplace in Anglican churches since medieval times. They traditionally consist of the pedestal (base), stand (column) topped by a sphere, and the desk (the eagle's outstretched wings) holding the open Bible. The Bible contains many references to the eagle, characterized as guide and protector. The eagle is also the symbol of St. John the Evangelist. Known for its ability to fly high and thus close to heaven, the eagle also represents the symbolic power to spread the word of God to the ends of the earth.

A fixture in the church since its earliest days is this ornately carved oak alms basin, which at Old Swedes consists of a globe on a pedestal. The alms basin features a substantial lock. An opening for donations is in the shape of a cross, and the top is carved with the words "Alms of thy goods." Giving alms, considered an act of virtue or charity, is a widespread practice in many different religions and cultures. Alms are given to meet the church's financial needs and support its ministry to the less fortunate. The alms basin is traditionally either near the altar or an entrance door; the Old Swedes alms basin is seen at left in the mid-1950s at the south door and below in 1934 at the bell tower door in a Historic American Buildings Survey photograph. (Below, Library of Congress, Prints & Photographs Division, HABS DEL, 2-WILM, 1-19.)

The Swedish priest primarily responsible for the construction of Old Swedes Church, Erik Björk, left Holy Trinity and the New Sweden colony after 17 years to become parish priest in Falun, Sweden. At the time, Falun was the site of the world's largest and most productive copper mine and a cornerstone of the 18th-century Swedish economy. Despite the fact that the colony had been lost to Sweden since 1655, Reverend Björk successfully appealed to the shareholders of the Stora Kopparberg Company (Great Copper Mountain Mining Company) to fund the gift of a silver chalice and paten to his former parish in Delaware, which he remembered with great fondness. These communion vessels, plus a wafer box, were manufactured in Gothenburg and sent to Wilmington in 1719. The chalice is inscribed with the date "1718" and the words *"Tag och drick: theta ar min blod."* (Take and drink; this is my blood.) The silver wafer box is inscribed "Trinity Church A.D. 1718."

This 1891 window in the sacristy honors the first pastor, Erik Björk. Tablet memorials also adorn the church walls. In 1885, a local newspaper described a marble tablet in the shape of a shield, surmounted by crossed swords and a knight's helmet dedicated to the memory of Civil War hero Capt. Richard Brindley. An 1899 tablet erected in memory of statesman Thomas F. Bayard is inscribed with the Ten Commandments.

Thomas F. Bayard commissioned this window on the southeast wall from the Louis Comfort Tiffany Studios in memory of his parents, James Asheton Bayard Jr. (1799–1880) and Anne Francis Bayard (1802–1864). It was installed in 1891. James Bayard served as a US senator from 1851 to 1864 and from 1867 to 1869. Thomas F. Bayard, one of the wealthier members of the parish, sought ways to benefit the church, the commissioning of memorial windows being one.

Pillars of their church and community, William and Margaret Forrest emigrated from Ireland in 1832, were married in the church in 1835, and are buried at Old Swedes. "Billy" Forrest, whose work life began at the du Pont powder works, opened a grocery store at Sixth and Poplar Streets in 1850; for years, the family lived close to the church at Eighth and Buttonwood Streets. Later, he started businesses as a carter, contractor, and builder while his wife ran the grocery. The September 21, 1886, *Daily Republican* reported that more than 2,000 attended her funeral, the line stretching from the church all the way to the Forrest residence. The nine-foot-tall Forrest window in her memory was manufactured by the J&R Lamb Co. of New York and was installed in 1889. William Forrest died in 1893.

The black walnut pulpit, in its original location, is elevated above the sanctuary floor. In Swedish churches of the era, the upraised pulpit affirmed the importance and authority of the priest. Its octagonal wood canopy, 16 feet high, is supported by an iron rod attached to a roof rafter.

One of the two stained glass windows unfortunately affected by the second-floor gallery addition, this window was installed in 1892 on the southwest wall. It was given in memory of Joseph Millikin by his mother and father. Richly colored, the window's design is thought to be based on an 1824 painting by German historical painter Heinrich Hofmann entitled *Childhood of Christ*.

Also obscured by the gallery floor structure, this window is dedicated to the memory of Ellen Vandever (1780–1855) by her daughter Catherine. The Vandever name goes back to the earliest days of the parish. Last to be installed in the church in 1897, it incorporates floral and religious motifs with a geometric border. It also features a six-pointed star, which in the Christian faith is one of the oldest symbols representing the Lord.

Directly behind the altar is the Breck window, installed in 1886. It was commissioned by the Breck family in honor of Jane Elizabeth Breck (1815–1884), the wife of Trinity Parish rector Rev. Charles Breck (1816–1891). As described in the September 25, 1886, Wilmington *Morning News*, "[T]he design gives the impression of an old portico. Through the opening of this portico . . . is a group, representing Christ blessing little children."

The massive windows on each wall of Old Swedes were originally small-paned, clear-glass casement windows based on traditional Swedish styles of construction in the late 16th and 17th centuries. They were later replaced in the mid-18th century by sash windows featuring larger panes with fanlight transoms. It is thought that the multi-light section of the Bayard window, seen here from the outside, is the only surviving example dating to that period.

At a special service in Old Swedes Church on January 22, 1950, the Swedish ambassador to the United States, Erik Boehman, presented the parish with an altar cloth whose central cross was embroidered by King Gustav Adolphus V. More than 600 people crowded into the church, including Right Rev. Arthur R. McKinstry, bishop of the Episcopal Diocese of Delaware; John Weldon, a vestryman of Old Swedes for nearly 30 years; and Rev. H. Edgar Hammond, Old Swedes vicar. The scarlet cloth is also embroidered with various decorations in gold. The ambassador told the assembled congregation of his gratitude for the contributions made in early American history by the Swedish forefathers and conveyed the wishes of the king that the ties between Sweden and the United States would become ever stronger. The altar cloth can be seen behind the ambassador.

The church is decorated for Christmas in this image from the 1950s. Traditional Swedish decorations are natural and simple: fresh greens and candles are always found in the church. Other traditions in the Christmas season include the centuries-old celebration of Sankta Lucia and, in the home, making straw ornaments and decorating the Christmas tree.

A very special occasion at Holy Trinity—the evening service held during the celebration of the 375th anniversary of New Sweden's founding—was attended by King Carl XVI Gustaf and Queen Silvia (first pew, at right) and Eero Heinäluoma, speaker of the Finnish parliament (first pew, at left). On the altar is the cloth embroidered by the king's great-grandfather.

This church chest dates from 1713, when church records indicate that it was a gift from Christian Jorasson. Made of walnut and pine, it has ball feet and hand-forged iron brackets on the sides and the bottom. The chest was used to store important documents, church valuables, and money. It has two keyholes, each requiring a different key as a means of security.

The key framed at left is said to be original to the church, fitted to the massive iron lock securing the first-floor south doors. Both the south doors and their hinges, which extend nearly the width of the doors, are original to the church. The south doors, which face the Christina River, were at one time the primary entrance to Holy Trinity.

The design of the sanctuary's barrel-vaulted ceiling can clearly be seen here. Both ceiling and walls are finished with painted white plaster. In the church's early days, men and women sat separately during services on either side of the church—men on the south side and women on the north, a common practice in Swedish churches. The first pew on the men's side was reserved for visitors of importance and on the women's side for strangers. Church records indicate that the central set of pews was reserved for those congregants who had given the most to the building of the church. The box pews of the first floor seen here were installed in 1899, exact copies of the original church pews of 1699. The pews of the second-floor gallery were added in 1774 and provided a template for reconstruction of the replacement pews.

The Gallery in "Old Swede's Church"

Wilmington native Robert Shaw (1859–1912) was a self-taught etcher and painter, well-known in his time. The meticulous detail of his drawings affords more modern historians pictorial evidence of places and buildings either changed or disappeared. His drawing of the south-side gallery steps shows how little has changed at Old Swedes.

Looking down the steps of the gallery gives a close-up view of the handwrought hinges of the pew boxes. Light from the Millikin stained glass window streams in at right. In 1801, the stovepipe from a stove in the west end of the church passed over the gallery, giving its occupants a great deal of warmth and as much smoke. It was one of two used for heating the church.

Five

THE 20TH CENTURY

One wonders where the photographer was standing to take this 1934 large-format photograph made for the Historic American Buildings Survey. Industrial Wilmington can be seen in the distance. The cupola, an 1803 addition, reflects the fashionable Georgian style of the period. Its roof is made of copper sheets rather than wood shingles like the main roof. (Library of Congress, Prints & Photographs Division, HABS DEL, 2-WILM, 1-18.)

Eager children line up outside the Christina Community Center's Seventh Street entrance in 1945. The *Trinity Code* newsletter of Trinity Church reported in May 1946 that more than 3,100 youngsters spent time at the center. Noting that participants included immigrants from a variety of countries as well as Native Americans, the *Trinity Code* remarked, "At the Center, everyone meets on common ground, and shares common interests and responsibilities."

Old Swedes Church can be seen in the background of this view of the newly completed Christina Playground (1947). The redevelopment of a triangular piece of land on Church Street next to the center property into an outdoor playground cost approximately $135,000. The playground provided the neighborhood much-needed open space for outdoor games, movies, plays, and concerts in the summer.

Tercentenary celebrations of the founding of New Sweden, which included the opening of Fort Christina State Park, brought a national spotlight to Old Swedes. Looking ahead to the 250th anniversary of the consecration of the church, prominent landscape designer Charles Gillette was commissioned to restore the burial ground. The restoration work included planting and trimming trees, regrading the property, planting ivy, building a brick wall next to the railroad, and paving the driveways and walkways of the churchyard with brick. Much to the dismay of some in the parish, Gillette's restoration also meant the removal of the 1847 Gothic arch marking the main entrance to the grounds. The work, funded by the Garden Club of Wilmington, was completed by 1948.

Disaster in the form of lightning struck Old Swedes on the morning of April 29, 1964. Many of the church's neighbors reported seeing a flash and hearing a "terrific bolt of thunder" about half an hour before the fire was reported. Despite the head start and the winds that day of up to 30 miles per hour, Wilmington firefighters were able to contain the blaze to the west end of the building. It was thought that lightning struck the needle point of the weather vane atop the church's copper-plated cupola, one of the highest points in the neighborhood. Smoke from the fire was visible from Market Street, 11 blocks away.

Water drips off the glass case of the model of the *Kalmar Nyckel* (Key of Kalmar) in front of the south porch after it was salvaged from the church. This ship, accompanied by the smaller *Fogel Grip*, carried Swedish colonists to the New World in 1638 and later, making four voyages in all. The scale model was a 1963 gift to the City of Wilmington from Kalmar, its sister city in Sweden, and is on permanent loan to Old Swedes.

Members of the parish and the rector, Rev. Percy F. Rex, watch as firefighters work to prevent the blaze from spreading to the sanctuary. The first alarm was called in around 10:00 a.m. by John Mosiej, who lived a block north of the church and who apparently saw smoke pouring from the building. Four fire engines and a ladder truck arrived on the scene shortly after. Wilmington fire chief Maurice K. Clark soon called for an additional two engines and a second ladder truck. "We had a job on our hands," he said, noting that it took 40 firefighters to bring the fire under control by 11:00 a.m., hampered by wind, rain, and the height of the roof.

Six hoses in all were hauled into the church, up to the gallery, and up the belfry stairway, in back of the organ (at right). Rev. H. Edgar Hammond, Trinity Parish historian and retired Old Swedes rector, praised the work of the city firemen. "They were careful. They tried to do as little damage as possible, and they laid tarpaulins where they could," he said.

The church's pipe organ, located in the center of the second-floor gallery, was heavily damaged by the fire. Its installation dated to 1909. The Austin Organ Company of Hartford, Connecticut, donated the church's current organ (Opus 2425) to aid in the restoration efforts in 1964. Replacing the pipes alone could have cost between $25,000 and $30,000.

A firefighter peers down from his perch in the belfry tower past hose line and ladder, framed by the charred timbers of Old Swedes' roof. The cupola is above his head. The foot-thick beams dated to the church's construction in 1698, though the roof's shingles, although made of wood, dated from the mid-20th century. The fire left gaping holes in the roof.

While damage to the church's roof was estimated at $75,000, the priceless relics within were undamaged. Soon after the fire was discovered, clergy, parishioners, and neighbors formed a bucket brigade to carry out the many items of historic value. First on the scene was Rev. James B. Prichard, vicar of Old Swedes, who ran into the church to scoop up the altar cloth made by Swedish king Gustavus Adolphus V and given to the church in 1950. Also rescued were the 1719 silver communion service, a heavy wooden money chest dating to the 1700s, and a wealth of historic paintings and photographs. Several hours after the fire was declared under control, firefighters were carting away burnt shingles and chunks of scorched wet plaster and sweeping several inches of water out of the church.

Father Prichard, Old Swedes vicar, walks through the scaffolding put up in the first phase of reconstruction. The roof was completely rebuilt with added steel reinforcements to the old rafters, which survived the fire. The interior had to be replastered and painted due to smoke damage. The work also included installation of a sprinkler system and lightning protectors. The work, which cost in excess of $100,000, was completed by December 1964. The building was insured. A service of thanksgiving to celebrate completion of the repairs was held in the church on December 5. While the work was ongoing, Holy Trinity's services had been held in the nearby Christina Community Center.

Proudly bearing the altar cloth embroidered by King Gustav Adolphus V, the altar in the 1960s was the marble-encased version created in the 1899 restoration. Like the original altar of 1699, this one is set flush against the east wall and surrounded by a chancel rail, which has a center opening the width of the main aisle.

In 1988, Homsey Architects of Wilmington undertook a significant modification to the church—the removal and replacement of the altar. The 1899 marble encasing the original altar was removed, and the altar itself was moved 28 inches from the wall. The marble panel bearing the names of the 10 Swedish priests who served Old Swedes was set in the floor behind the altar.

The second stage of the altar replacement project entailed constructing a new walnut altar, four feet wide by two feet, three inches deep and three feet, five inches high. In front of the chancel, at the head of the main aisle, is the gravestone of Rev. Peter Tranberg, pastor from 1742 to 1748. He is one of 11 buried underneath the church itself.

The Swedish cultural tradition celebrating Sankta Lucia, the bearer of light, and the beginning of the holiday season is a beloved tradition at Old Swedes Church, annually sponsored by the Delaware Swedish Colonial Society. Crowds gather in the candlelit church to see the procession of St. Lucia, her attendants, star boys, and the Christmas elves. All sing the Lucia song and Christmas hymns in Swedish.

Wearing the traditional wreath of greens and candles, this Lucia—who likely got her start as one of the red-clad *tomten*, or Christmas elves, years ago in a previous Lucia celebration—proudly bears the offering of *lussekatter* (Lucia cats), sweet saffron buns. She is followed by her white-gowned attendants (*tärnor*) and star boys (*stjärngossar*), wearing cone-shaped hats and carrying star-adorned sticks.

A volunteer cleans gravestones in the 1980s. The churchyard, with its many trees, takes a great deal of maintenance. The gravestones, numbering over 1,200, are subject to damage from weather, biological growth, settling ground, and accidents—falling tree limbs, for example. Old Swedes has benefited from the volunteer efforts of Trinity Parish members, Scout troops, and individuals who have a great affection for the site.

On its first-ever tour of North America, the Tapiola Chamber Choir (Tapiolan Kamarikuoro) performed at Old Swedes Church on June 23, 2015. The tour program featured Finnish choral music old and new, celebrating the 150th anniversary of the birth of Jean Sibelius, Finland's best-known composer. The choir's adventurous programming, diverse repertoire, and ambitious recording schedule have received critical acclaim and awards in Finland and abroad.

The amphitheater on the historic site property is used for concerts and open space. It contains a labyrinth, the creation of longtime Old Swedes parishioner Max Dooley. Inspired by a visit to Grace Cathedral in San Francisco, he sought to bring the same tranquil experience to the concrete circle that resembles a stage in the site's amphitheater. Interviewed some years ago, Dooley said, "I would describe the design as a series of seven concentric circular pathways, truncated into quadrants, ultimately leading into then out of the circular center. The entrance is also the exit . . . two paths as you are coming in and going out. It is a spiritual thing which cuts across all religions, but it has to do with how the individual feels along the way." A group of volunteers recently repainted the labyrinth lines.

Open hearth cooking is demonstrated in the Hendrickson House by interpreter Susan Plaisted on Colonists' Day. Plaisted demonstrates Colonial American foodways of the 17th and 18th centuries using period practices, methods, and receipts (recipes). Here, she rolls out the traditional Swedish *knäckebröd* (rye crisp bread), a round flat loaf with a hole in the middle. In colonial days, it was dried in the hearth and stored on long poles hung from the ceiling.

Colonial reenactors are part of the pageantry of special events such as Colonists' Day at Old Swedes. These three men portray soldiers in the 17th-century Swedish army. Swedish military uniforms were standardized in the late 1600s; each regiment was dressed in specific colors. These soldiers' headgear is the *karpus*, a circular, heavy woolen or fur-lined bonnet worn extensively by the rank and file in the infantry.

The descendants of Dr. Timen Stiddem gather at Old Swedes for a family reunion. Dr. Stiddem was a barber-surgeon employed by the Swedish crown who made four expeditions to America, including the Swedes' first voyage in 1638. He later settled in Wilmington and is recognized as the first doctor in Delaware. There are an estimated 64 Stidhams (the name is variously spelled) buried at Old Swedes.

Hendrickson House hosts a demonstration of colonial-period painting by artist Kevin O'Malley, who creates historical drawings and portraits in graphite, wash, and oil. For historical accuracy, O'Malley makes his own brushes and paints. "The history of America has always been a unique source of inspiration. At Old Swedes and in other parts of this area there are stories of both local and national interest to be discovered," he said.

Six

CHRISTINA COMMUNITY CENTER AND THE HENDRICKSON HOUSE

This Gothic Revival archway, originally freestanding, was built at the northwest corner of the property by 1847 to serve as the primary entrance to the churchyard. In 1887, a parish house was appended to the rear (or church side) of the arch (at left). Accommodations for the vicar and sexton were built in and attached to the other side of the arch (at right).

This view from the churchyard side of the arch is looking out toward the corner of North Church and Seventh Streets. The door on the left led to the rector's office. The brick parish house is seen at right in this early-1940s photograph. The arch, which when built boasted a crenelated roof and two tall spires, was intended to establish an impressive entrance for the newly improved church.

Prompted by influential members of the parish, the burial ground was restored to commemorate the 250th anniversary of the consecration of the church. The work was also part of an ambitious plan to build a community center on the property, requiring a complete redesign of the churchyard. This 1945 photograph looks north up the wide carriage path toward the arch on the corner of Church and Seventh Streets.

Old Swedes' youth organization–sponsored basketball teams competed against other Wilmington teams in a gymnasium in the parish house. The 1913–1914 team included, from left to right, (first row) Willard Schaffer, Fritz Schaffer, Warren Cooper, and Roy Smith; (second row) Gallorick Mallory, Oscar Moore, Reverend Woven, and two unidentified. The team was named Orient, as the players hailed from the east side of the city. (Robert Smith, Roy Smith's grandson.)

Plans for a new community center originally called for a two-story building at the corner of Church and Sixth Streets. The new center would offer a range of social and educational services to "The Old Swedes Area," a 173-block area where an estimated 4,736 children under the age of 18 lived. A 1951 article in the *Witness* noted that "the old church at the water's edge now stands in a congested, partly outmoded section of the city . . . prey to racial tensions, cultural and national groups in social and economic competition and very thickly populated." Until sufficient funds were raised for the new building, the project leaders turned to the old parish house as a temporary home for the community center. The existing building was renovated and an addition constructed. The 1847 arch and the buildings attached to it (parsonage, rector's office, and sexton's house) were demolished to make room for construction of the addition.

In 1945, church and civic leaders chartered a corporation, the Christina Community Center of Old Swedes Inc., to lead the project and raise the necessary funds. Pierre S. du Pont III served as president. Rev. H. Edgar Hammond, then vicar of Old Swedes, served as secretary to the campaign committee. In a fundraising brochure he wrote, "Over the last sixteen years, [Old Swedes'] 'Adventure in Community' has grown under volunteer leadership . . . Educational in nature, the program is now divided into 28 activity groups for youths of the area—teaching moral and ethical requirements of good citizenship without religious denominational or political bias. Again, Old Swedes stands as the symbol of community—with a future role beyond that of an historic shrine."

When construction was completed, the resulting building housed a gymnasium with locker rooms, a kitchen and snack bar, a library and reading room, a large open recreation hall, a woodworking shop, club rooms for Girl Scouts and Boy Scouts and men's and women's groups, a music room, and a craft room for ceramics, sewing, weaving, and metalworking. Its programs offered recreation, vocational guidance, health care, cultural activities, and a variety of arts programs, including drawing, painting, and instrumental and vocal music groups. Instead of a new building at Sixth and Church Streets, since sufficient funds were not raised, a playground was designed and installed in the two blocks adjoining the church property.

THE GRAVEYARD ARCHWAY.

This more romantic view of the archway over the main entrance to the churchyard by Wilmington artist Robert Shaw was published in the 1899 booklet issued to commemorate the 200th anniversary of Old Swedes' consecration. Shaw contributed a dozen drawings to the booklet, documenting in finely drawn detail current and historic views of the church, tombs, and churchyard. In this drawing, Shaw accurately captures the existing buildings, including the two-chimneyed, three-story brick rowhouse across the street, which is framed in the arch. He manages, however, to give the scene a more pastoral air and makes the concrete buildings more charming than they likely were in reality.

Members of the Young Men's and Young Women's Choirs of Holy Trinity process to the church as part of the opening ceremonies of the Christina Community Center on March 29, 1948. Old Swedes had partnered with the YMCA since 1915 to provide vital programs for youth in the East Side, an aging, congested neighborhood with its share of racial, ethnic, and cultural tensions.

Opening ceremonies for the Christina Community Center were broadcast by local NBC affiliate WDEL. Dignitaries attending are, from left to right, Rev. Edgar Hammond, vicar of Old Swedes; Rev. Donald W. Mayberry, rector of Trinity Episcopal; Charles Davis, center director; Right Reverend Arthur R. McKinstry, bishop of the Episcopal Diocese of Delaware (speaking); Joseph S. Wilson, mayor of Wilmington; and P.S. du Pont III, a founder of the center and president of its board of directors.

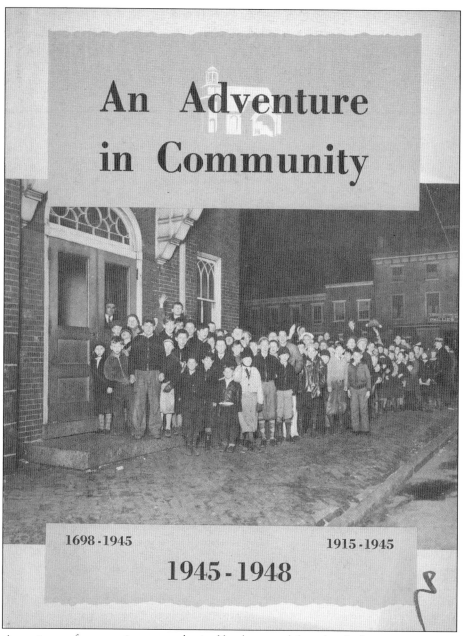

An Adventure in Community

1698 - 1945   1915 - 1945

1945 - 1948

The importance of community was emphasized by the center's board and administration. In 1945, a group of civic and church leaders, led by P.S. du Pont III, created the Christina Community Center of Old Swedes Inc. for the purpose of creating better facilities for the increasingly popular programs cosponsored by the church and the YMCA. That year, a census of the immediate neighborhood found that it contained 3,536 children enrolled in public and parochial schools and an additional estimated 1,200 preschool children. The only recreational space prior to the construction of the playground consisted of two small city parks about a block each in size. The corporation gradually acquired two adjacent blocks of rowhouses along Church Street; after the residents of those 28 houses were resettled and the buildings demolished, the land was regraded and an outdoor playground with swings and slides was put in place.

According to church publications, in 1948, the center's operating budget was included in the Community Fund (Red Feather) campaign in Wilmington, which thereafter largely underwrote the program. The balance of its budget was provided by the women's club of Trinity Episcopal, which had founded the original center to provide activities for Swedish and Polish immigrant families. The women's club's Christmas Shop presented an annual watercolor exhibition in the Hotel du Pont lobby. Each year, an artist represented in the show donated a picture to be displayed in the center. The Bayard T. Berndt historical depiction of Old Swedes Church still on display in the building is one of those.

One of many family events held in the large recreation hall was square dancing, as seen here in 1962. A variety of cultural programs were held at the center. A steel drum ensemble performed in 1968. A demonstration dinner of East and West African dishes was held in 1981. Arts classes offered in 1982 included calligraphy, gospel music, instrumental music, voice, dance, photography, drama, domestic arts, pottery, drawing, and painting. (Christina Cultural Arts Center.)

The second-floor gymnasium was used for choir practice, dances, musical performances, and music appreciation programs as well as athletic and recreational activities. The community center has now evolved into the Christina Cultural Arts Center. Its mission was redefined in 1969, according to its website at ccacde.org, "To serve as a community-based arts center with an emphasis on preserving African American cultural heritage." The Christina Cultural Arts Center is now located in downtown Wilmington. (Christina Cultural Arts Center.)

The community center offered services, programs, and activities for all ages, from health clinics to this 1964 kindergarten class, to high school–age students seeking individual, vocational, and educational counseling services in addition to athletics and classes in arts, crafts, and hobbies. Employment help was also available. Leadership opportunities for boys and girls included senior and junior government councils, the Vicar's Club (junior leaders), and senior and junior camp clubs. (Christina Cultural Arts Center.)

Members of a Boy Scout troop gather in 1960; they are reading about Brotherhood Week. The community center hosted several Cub Scout packs as well as two Girl Scout troops. After the community center program was renamed and moved, the building was again repurposed, though it is still affectionately referred to as "C3." Part of the building currently houses a day care; other spaces are used for meetings and exhibitions. (Christina Cultural Arts Center.)

The Going Home Chorus, a large ensemble directed by Elizabeth Johnson, sang for elderly patients in hospitals and in churches, senior centers, and other institutions, reaching out to the lonely, isolated, and ill. The singers, whose intent was to offer encouragement, religious support, and a positive line of communication, are shown rehearsing in the center in 1970. (Christina Cultural Arts Center.)

East Side neighborhood families had their taxes prepared by personnel from the Internal Revenue Service in the Christina Community Center gallery in 1973. The community also gathered for events such as family suppers, repertory theater performances, art exhibitions, music appreciation programs, and mother and daughter fashion shows sponsored by the Mothers' Sewing Class. (Christina Cultural Arts Center.)

One of the oldest extant 18th-century Swedish-built structures in the country, the Hendrickson House was originally located in Ridley Township, Pennsylvania. It was built sometime between 1722 and 1746 by Catherine Hendrickson, widow of Anders (Andrew) Hendrickson. The Durborow family lived in the former farmhouse, pictured here in 1880. Thanks to Paul James Weaver Jr., the young ladies are identified as, from left to right, Eva Anna, Andrewia, and Sylvania. They were the children of Joseph (1858–1928) and Frederika (Schrader, 1854–1942) Durborow. A brother, not pictured, was Joseph B. Jr. Paul Weaver, who donated the framed photograph to the Old Swedes Foundation in 2008, is the great-grandson of Eva Anna (Durborow) Wilkin. At the time, the house was owned and rented out by the Ward family, who operated a quarry and brickmaking operation on the property. In 1918, the entire property was sold to the Baldwin Locomotive Company, which left the house unoccupied.

Andrew Hendrickson inherited a 154-acre tract of land on the northeast bank of Crum Creek in Ridley Township upon the death of his father, Hendrick Johnsson, in 1676. By 1691, he had married and begun to develop the land, probably building a log dwelling for his growing family. After his first wife died in 1702, Hendrickson married his second wife, Catherine, and with her had six children. The stone house pictured here was built by Catherine sometime after Andrew's death in 1722. The Hendricksons successfully farmed their land, raising livestock and grains, growing orchard fruits and vegetables, and fishing in the local creeks using a seine net. Andrew's estate inventory following his death listed 5 horses, 25 head of cattle, 23 sheep, farming tools, household goods including three spinning wheels, pewter ware, chests, and books. Catherine Hendrickson did not remarry; with her children, she continued to manage the farm, and sometime in the early 1700s built a new stone house in the Swedish style.

The original section of the house, in this view of the front, is marked by the door flanked by two windows at left. The hall-parlor plan of the house consisted of one large room on the first floor used in the family's daily activities and one bedroom above, under a Swedish gambrel roof. There were just four windows, and a cellar to store food. At the time, it would have been regarded as the home of a well-to-do, respectable family. By the 1800s, the property included a sawmill and a stone quarry. Ownership had passed from the Hendrickson family through a number of hands, and the house was often rented out. An addition was built on the east end between 1834 and 1842, which was likely meant to provide office space and housing for the quarry manager. Renovations at the time included enlarging the windows and adding the dormers. At various times, the house boasted a porch across its entire front, a small lean-to–type addition on one end, and a coat of whitewash.

The Baldwin Locomotive Company owned the property from 1918 to 1956, leaving the house unoccupied. Years of neglect took a toll, as did a serious fire in 1924. Baldwin made repairs to the exterior in 1925–1926, but otherwise did not maintain it. By the time the property was sold to the Vertol Aircraft Corporation in 1958, the building was in serious disrepair. Vertol planned to redevelop the land, which required demolition of the Hendrickson House. Local residents, preservationists, and historians raised the alarm in the press and made appeals to elected officials. In July 1958, the Old Swedes Foundation offered to move the house to the churchyard to serve as a historical museum, and Vertol agreed to donate it. The Haddock Construction Company was hired for the disassembling and reconstruction, and the firm of Whiteside Moeckel and Carbonell was hired as architects.

At midpoint in the deconstruction of the building, architectural details such as an enclosed winding staircase, beams, and wooden board-and-batten shutters were revealed. Dismantling of the Hendrickson House began at the top, with removal of the shingled roof. Its wooden framework was next to go, later replaced with new beams, joists, and rafters in its new location.

Reduced to a one-story shell, the Hendrickson House is pictured in 1958. Many of the beams damaged in the 1924 fire could not be reused. Enough were salvaged, however, to be used as patterns for duplication. Window frames, sashes, exterior doors and frames, and dormers all had to be newly built in the reconstruction.

On October 21, 1959, groundbreaking ceremonies for the Hendrickson House's new location on the grounds of Old Swedes were held. According to newspaper reports, the noise of traffic on Church Street (behind the group) drowned out much of the ceremony, but transcripts were provided. From left to right are Harry Haskell, Old Swedes Foundation board member; Dr. John S. Reese IV, chairman of the Hendrickson House Committee and Holy Trinity senior warden; Ross M. Lanius II, Holy Trinity junior warden; Thomas F. Bayard III, Old Swedes Foundation board chairman; Rev. H. Edgar Hammond, vicar of Holy Trinity; Rev. Percy Rex, rector of Holy Trinity; David P. Buckson, lieutenant governor of Delaware (with shovel); Rev. Benjamin Narbeth, assistant rector of Holy Trinity; and Very Rev. Lloyd Gressle, dean of the Cathedral Church of St. John. Father Hammond turned the first shovelful of dirt, and Lieutenant Governor Buckson presented a Swedish flag and citation from the people of Gothenburg, Sweden, as a gesture of goodwill.

A basement was dug before the structure was rebuilt in its new location, as the building was intended to serve as museum, church offices, and archive. This pile of rubble is the beginnings of the foundation, in a view looking south toward the railroad tracks. The team overseeing the project realized early on that the only materials salvageable for the reconstruction were the masonry walls, some wooden elements, and pieces of iron hardware. Much of the original interior woodwork and hardware had been lost to vandals and unauthorized salvagers before the house was moved to Delaware. In the first phase of the project, from October 1959 to February 1960, a section of the stone wall enclosing the churchyard was demolished to clear space for the house and give access to the work crews, and the walls and roof were then reconstructed over the newly excavated basement.

Shown in its new site, the Hendrickson House was located to the west of the Christina Community Center (at left) and just outside the stone wall built around the church property in 1837. The signs advertise the construction firm and architects for the project. Also hired was a Winterthur-trained historic architect, Robert L. Raley, as an expert in the Colonial period who could ensure the appropriate look of the reconstructed building. He designed replacement elements such as hardware, and found a variety of materials like floorboards and paneling salvaged from demolished houses of the period in the Delaware Valley, Hudson Valley, and New England. He also produced drawings for the staircases and plans for lighting and outlets for heating. The reconstruction was essentially complete by the summer of 1961. The final phase, re-landscaping the area around the building and constructing a parking area, was completed by landscape architect Robert Wheelwright of the Philadelphia firm Wheelwright and Stevenson.

The Hendrickson House's addition, which allowed a reconfiguration of the living spaces inside, is estimated to have been built between 1834 and 1842. The joint of the two sections—original building on the right, addition on the left—is seen clearly here. The roof had most recently been replaced after the 1924 fire. A new roof of hand-split cedar shingles was one of the final elements of the first phase of rebuilding.

Carpenters are hard at work framing the new gambrel roof. The building's brick chimneys were replaced with stone in the reconstruction on the recommendation of historic architect Robert Raley. It is unknown whether the brick upper segments were original to the house. The flooring was entirely replaced with antique pine flooring salvaged from old buildings in Massachusetts.

Standing in front of the massive fireplace opening within the interior of the partly reconstructed Hendrickson House are members of the building committee meeting with representatives of the architectural firm overseeing the project. From left to right are Old Swedes board president Thomas F. Bayard, architect William Moeckel, David Stockwell, historic architect Robert Raley, and committee member Marian Warner. The hearth, which had been reduced in size many years earlier, was restored to its original appearance. The original mantel and fireplace surround had been partly plastered over but was uncovered and restored. The chimney lintel, according to the architects, was a huge oak timber measuring about 18 inches square and eight feet long. The mantel, surround, and lintel were the only wood elements salvaged before the house was disassembled. Those elements were reinstalled in their original location, the opening seen in the background above. The small window in the end wall within the hearth seen below is also original to the building.

This view of the Hendrickson House interior shows the original main room as it appeared shortly after the building was opened to the public in 1961. Period furnishings, none original to the house, were added to give an idea of the plain yet serviceable goods of the Hendrickson family. The inventory of Andrew Hendrickson's estate made following his death in 1722 lists four feather beds and furnishings, three chairs, three spinning wheels, and three chests. It also listed books, a gun, two saddles and bridles, fire tongs, two candlesticks, three iron pots, and pewter ware in the form of ten plates, six large dishes, two small dishes, four pots, and two basins. Today, the main room includes a large wood *kas*, a cabinet common to the 17th and 18th centuries, with two doors and a drawer; a spinning wheel; cooking pots and utensils; several chairs; and a c. 1685 board and trestle table donated by H. Rodney Sharp. The original will of Andrew Hendrickson is displayed on one wall.

All new beams, rafters, and wood shingles were crafted for the reconstruction. Note the butt joint between the original Hendrickson House at right and the later addition at left, which can be seen clearly in this photograph of the finished reconstruction. This view shows the stone wall of the west side of the building (originally the rear of the house), facing Church Street. It is likely that the stone used for the walls was quarried on the Crum Creek property where the house was originally built. Some stones still bear fragments of the whitewash that was applied early in the 20th century. The primary cornerstones of the building appear to be in their original locations based on comparison with the earliest photographs available. Records in the Old Swedes archive note that each stone was labeled so that it could be reset exactly where it was in the original building. Seen below is the original front, now facing the church.

Seven

NOTABLE IN THE
BURIAL GROUND

It is estimated that the burial ground is the final resting place of more than 12,000 individuals. Early burials were marked with stones or wooden crosses, or left unmarked, leaving no trace. There are currently 1,286 markers of various ages, shapes, sizes, and condition within the three-plus-acre churchyard. Records indicate that there are 11 people interred under the floor of the church itself, the earliest dating to 1709.

The oldest extant gravestone in the burial ground is believed to be that of William Vandever, who died in October 1719. The shape of the stone and the style of the engraved letters with a suitably solemn message is characteristically Colonial. There are more than 40 members of the Vandever family interred at Old Swedes. Vandever, a church warden, donated stone from his land to build the walls of the church.

Known as "cradle graves" or "bedstead monuments," this type of Victorian-era marker is composed of a headstone, footstone, and side molding. Despite the name, they were not just for children; adult graves were also marked in this manner. The space between the curbed sides was filled with blanket planting—flowers, grasses, or bushes. These two mark the final resting place of Charles F. (1879–1886) and Alfred H. Barney (1889–1893).

A striking monument in the burial ground is that of the O'Daniel family. This tall marker is topped by a statue of an angel. Angels represent messengers between God and man as well as guardians for the deceased. The wreath in the center of the stone represents victory in death. Buried here are William F. O'Daniel (1807–1863); his first wife, Sarah (1810–1844); his second wife, Elizabeth (1818–1875); and 10 children.

An angel likewise adorns the imposing Forrest family marker, a pedestal monument topped by a column. William G. Forrest dedicated the stained glass window on the northeast wall of the church in memory of his wife. Both emigrants from Donegal, Ireland, they were longtime parishioners at Old Swedes.

Right Rev. Bishop Alfred Lee (1807–1887) was born in Cambridge, Massachusetts, and studied law at Harvard. He practiced law in Norwich, Connecticut, from 1831 to 1833. After receiving his call to ministry, he attended New York's General Theological Seminary and was ordained a priest in 1838. In 1841, at age 34, he was consecrated as the first bishop of the Diocese of Delaware. Prior to Lee's consecration, affairs of the Episcopate had been administered by assistant bishops of Pennsylvania. As bishop, Lee worked to build churches and congregations in Delaware, served as rector of St. Andrew's in Wilmington, and was active in social issues of the time. He was elected to the Wilmington Board of Education, served as president of the Delaware Association for the Education of the Colored People, and was president of the Delaware Association for the Relief of Sick and Wounded Soldiers during the Civil War. A number of his family members and descendants are buried here in the Lee plot.

Among the more elaborate monuments in the burial ground are those in the southwest corner: Bauduy, Deschapelle, and Garesche. These wealthy French families fled the 1791 rebellion of the enslaved population in the French colony of St. Domingue (now Haiti) and relocated to Wilmington. Peter Bauduy (1769-1833) was an early partner of Eleuthère Irénée du Pont and is said to be the architect of Old Town Hall in Wilmington.

Reflecting the influence of the Egyptian Revival movement of the early 19th century, these singularly shaped grave markers are less commonly found. The obelisk, less costly than sculpted monuments of an equal size, was thought to be tasteful, associated with ancient greatness, even patriotic. The Washington Monument is perhaps the largest example. The pyramid seen here marks the resting place of William Hammon (1752-1816) and William Hammon Jr. (1798-1805).

Florence (Bayard) Hilles (1866–1954) was a founder of the National Woman's Party and a leader in the suffrage movement. Wearing the tricolor suffrage sash, she was a principal speaker on the 1916 Suffrage Special nationwide journey, where she led dramatic open-air meetings to generate support for national suffrage. She endured the opposition of her family, arrest, and imprisonment for the cause. The Florence Bayard Hilles Research Library in Washington, DC, houses the archives of the National Woman's Party.

Among the most influential families in Delaware, the Bayards were prominent in Democratic politics for generations. More than 20 members of the family lie in the vault enclosed by cast-iron fencing on the south side of the church: senators, diplomats, lieutenant governors, activists, and lawyers, along with their children and spouses.

Scientist, explorer, entrepreneur, author, and university professor, William Hypolitus Keating (1799–1840) was a remarkable man. Educated at the University of Pennsylvania (bachelor of arts, 1816), he studied mining in France and Switzerland before joining the faculty at his alma mater in 1822 as professor of chemistry and mineralogy (1822–1828). A capable field geologist, Keating accompanied Stephen Long's second expedition in 1823. His work with Long resulted in one of the first topographic and mineralogical surveys of the Great Lakes; he compiled and published the results as *Narrative of an Expedition to the Source of St. Peter's River*. Keating was a leading member of the Academy of Natural Sciences of Philadelphia and the American Philosophical Society, and a cofounder of the Franklin Institute (1824). He also studied law and was engaged in a number of business enterprises. He died in London, England, on March 17, 1840, while negotiating a mortgage loan for the Philadelphia & Reading Railroad Co., and is buried at Old Swedes with his wife and daughter. (Historical and Interpretive Collections of the Franklin Institute, Philadelphia, Pennsylvania.)

The grave marker of James Platt (d. 1848) bears a bas-relief carving of a weeping willow tree. Very popular in the early 19th century, the weeping willow's obvious meaning relates to grief or mourning. It carries another meaning: In many cultures, the willow is a symbol of immortality since it grows quickly almost anywhere. Willows have connections to ancient Greece, carried by the poet Orpheus and planted by the sorceress Circe.

There are numerous examples of the table tomb at Old Swedes, including some that have sunk to ground level. The table tomb is traditionally six-legged, erected over the gravesite, and supports a stone tablet that carries an inscription. These types of markers are very susceptible to weathering and damage due to their design and amount of surface exposure.

Sven Colsberg served Holy Trinity as bell ringer, schoolmaster, and parish clerk; he read homilies at services, ferried the priests across the river to preach to other congregations, and painted the church doors and windows. He died in 1710. About 310 years later, this top of an onion bottle bearing his name and the date 1706 was found along the shores of the Delaware River and eventually traced to Old Swedes.

Among the military heroes buried here is Maj. Peter Jaquett (1754–1834), a distinguished officer of the Delaware militia in the American Revolution. Under Gen. George Washington, he fought in every military engagement that took place in the mid-Atlantic states, numbering more than 30. Born at Long Hook Farm just south of Wilmington, he returned to farm after his military career. Here, his grave is visited by a Revolutionary War reenactor.

In the fall of 1923, Most Rev. Nathan Söderblom, archbishop of the Church of Sweden, was on an extensive preaching tour of the United States, a highlight of which was a visit to Holy Trinity on November 16, 1923. He remarked that any Swede would recognize its resemblance to Swedish churches from the Middle Ages (whose main entrance was invariably on the south side and the sacristy on the north side near the altar). An advocate for peace and practical cooperation among churches, the archbishop was awarded the Nobel Peace Prize in 1930. Pictured outside Old Swedes are, from left to right, Rev. Dr. Frederick M. Kirkus, rector of Trinity Episcopal Church; Grant Hultgren, United Lutheran Church publishing director; A. William Oestergren, a native of Sweden residing in Wilmington; John Söderblom, the archbishop's son; Reverend Söderblom; Rev. Robert Bell, vicar of Old Swedes; and Rev. Frederick Doerr, pastor of St. Stephen's Lutheran Church.

Eight

OLD SWEDES IN ART AND ARTIFACTS

Holy Trinity made of paper—this is one of the more unusual artifacts in the foundation's archives. Perhaps inspired during a fourth-grade trip to Old Swedes to learn about the early history of Delaware, a now-anonymous youngster created this paper model of the church's interior in the 1960s. The attention to detail earns its maker an "A."

Wilmington native Howard Pyle is considered the "Father of American Illustration" for his superb and prolific work as an artist, writer, and teacher. He taught more than 200 students at Drexel Institute, then in his Wilmington school, including such artists as N.C. Wyeth, Maxfield Parrish, Violet Oakley, Frank Schoonover, and Jessie (Willcox) Smith. An inspiring teacher, he accepted any talented student free of charge at his house and the summer studio he opened in Chadds Ford, Pennsylvania. Pyle was a consummate storyteller whose dramatic, vibrant pictures of legends, myths, and historical events brought him international recognition. He wrote and illustrated his own stories, beginning with *The Merry Adventures of Robin Hood* in 1883, and is credited with creating the popular image of pirate dress. This illustration was used for sketches he wrote entitled "By Land and Sea" for *Harper's New Monthly Magazine*, December 1895. (*The Sailor's Wedding*, 1895. Howard Pyle (1853–1911). Oil on illustration board. Delaware Art Museum, Museum Purchase, 1912.)

This deerskin leather postcard was donated to the Old Swedes Foundation by Jim Crothers, who discovered the postcard in his late father's papers. J. Alexander Crothers was, early in his career, assistant manager of the Wilmington Marine Terminal. The postcard was made by the Hy-Sil Manufacturing Company, the oldest gift wrap manufacturer in the United States, which began producing leather postcards in Boston, Massachusetts, in 1903.

Issued to celebrate the 300th anniversary of the founding of New Sweden, this 30 *öre* postage stamp was one of a series that also featured portraits of Queen Christina of Sweden (1626-1689), the New Sweden colony's first governor Peter Minuit, the *Kalmar Nyckel*, Swedish settlers, and Native Americans. *Nya Sverige Minnet* translates literally to "New Sweden Memory."

This wooden architect's model donated to Old Swedes is undated. Its details are faithful, such as the shingled jerkinhead roof with a hipped gable at the east end, the two north porches and the south porch with exterior staircase, the arched windows of the church and doors of the bell tower, and the bell tower's cupola with bell inside. The model can be disassembled but fits together neatly. The form and detailing of the actual church may be characterized as English colonial, due in no small part to the English artisans who built it, such as mason and bricklayer Joseph Yard and carpenter and joiner John Harrison, both of Philadelphia.

Artist Robert Shaw (1859–1912), a Wilmington native, created a series of etchings depicting historic landmarks of colonial America, published by the United States Historical Society. Inspired by local landscapes, landmarks, and architecture, the meticulously detailed renderings of this mostly self-taught artist are an important record of life in turn-of-the-20th-century Delaware. The remarque at bottom right is a bust of Rev. Erik Tobias Björk. (Old Swedes Foundation archives, gift of Margaret Springer Denham.)

Strange As It Seems, a syndicated cartoon feature published from 1928 to 1970, was similar to *Ripley's Believe It Or Not*. Created by John Hix, *Strange As It Seems* featured Old Swedes twice—the oldest church in the country standing as built and still in use, and the oldest church pulpit in the United States. Hix was notable for his strict standard that every fact be verified by a minimum of three sources.

The above image of the church has appeared on plates, cups, spoons, banners, postcards, and more. There is a remarkable variety of souvenir plates featuring Old Swedes, dating to the early 19th century. It is known that this example is from the mid-1800s by the original small-paned window on the south side of the church. Below, produced by Spode for the tercentenary celebration in 1938, this depiction of Old Swedes on a 10.5-inch porcelain plate made in England is one of a series of six. The set features historic and notable locations in Delaware, including the Old Court House, New Castle (1732); Old State House, Dover (1791); Old Town Hall, Wilmington (1798); Old College, University of Delaware (1834); and Zwaanendael House, Lewes (1931).

Entitled "WPA Painting in Progress," this photograph was the work of Willard Stewart, the primary photographer for the Delaware Federal Writers' Project who photographed numerous Delaware buildings and landscapes for the Works Progress Administration (WPA) and the Historic American Buildings Survey (HABS). The mural depicts the landing of the Swedes in 1638. (GRA 139, Willard Stewart Photographs of Delaware, Special Collections, University of Delaware Library, Museums and Press, Newark, Delaware.)

When it was finished, the WPA painting showing Old Swedes Church on high ground above the Christina River (with modern-day buildings in the background) was placed over the entrance to the WPA's administrative offices in Wilmington at 518 North King Street. Many WPA artworks graced government facilities; unfortunately, this one has been removed. (GRA 139, Willard Stewart Photographs of Delaware, Special Collections, University of Delaware Library, Museums and Press, Newark, Delaware.)

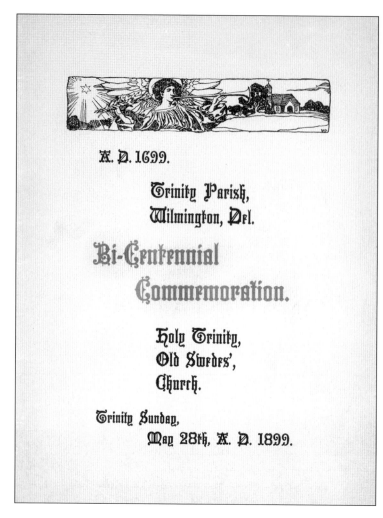

The headpiece of this commemorative program for the bicentennial celebration of the church's consecration was commissioned in 1899 from renowned American illustrator Howard Pyle. Pyle, who had a great affection for the old church, interestingly placed what may be the angel Gabriel with a bright star in front of the church. Holy Trinity has inspired artists such as Pyle, Andrew Wyeth, Robert Shaw, Bayard T. Berndt, and Peter Hurd.

OLD SWEDES' CHURCH : 1699

A young Andrew Wyeth drew Old Swedes Church as he imagined it looked in 1699. This sketch and several others by Wyeth and his father, N.C. Wyeth, were included in *The Delaware Tercentenary Almanack* (1937), a historical timeline published as part of the celebration of the 300th anniversary of the Swedes landing in the New World. (© 2023 Wyeth Foundation for American Art/Artists Rights Society, New York.)

Nine

ROYAL VISITS AND
NATIONAL STATUS

Intrepid members of the Justis family, descended from New Sweden colonists, canoe the Christina River with a homemade sign to welcome Crown Prince Bertil during his visit to Fort Christina State Park in March 1963. The prince's first visit at the age of 26 came during the tercentenary celebration. "I am reminded of the magnificent events of 25 years ago," he remarked in 1963. "The atmosphere of friendship is the same."

Swedish crown prince Gustaf Adolf (center) and his wife, Louise Mountbatten (at left), are pictured at the church door after a tour on May 31, 1926, with Rev. Robert Bell, Old Swedes vicar. The prince would later become King Gustaf VI Adolf in 1950. His wife was born a princess of the German house of Battenberg; she was the great-granddaughter of Queen Victoria and niece of the empress of Russia.

ADMIT

TO

Old Swedes Churchyard

MAY 31st, 1926

Prince Gustaf Adolf and Louise Mountbatten visited Old Swedes during the first leg of a lengthy tour around the world to promote Swedish interests. According to local news, the prince and princess were surprised by the young daughter of a Swedish woman who, evading the guards, rushed out of the crowd at the Wilmington train station to present the princess with a large bouquet of American Beauty roses tied with blue and yellow ribbons.

Swedish princesses Birgitta, age 23 (left), and Desiree, age 22 (center), visited Old Swedes in 1960. The elder sisters of Sweden's current King Carl XVI Gustav, they were received at Holy Trinity by Rev. Edgar Hammond, vicar (right). Their 10-day US tour included a Swedish ball in Philadelphia, a visit to the United Nations, and a reception given by the Swedish community in New York City.

Princesses Birgitta and Desiree charmed Wilmington in 1960. Here in the churchyard, they are presented with flowers by the daughters of Mr. and Mrs. Thomas F. Bayard III, Elizabeth du Pont Bayard and Ellen Lee Bayard. Thomas Bayard was president of the Old Swedes Foundation. The *Wilmington Morning News* reported, "The princesses practice a close-to-the-people kind of royalty, sometimes serving as teachers in Stockholm schools."

Crown Prince Bertil of Sweden (far right) is pictured at the rededication of Fort Christina Park in March 1963 to mark its designation as a national historic landmark. In Wilmington, he gave four speeches in three days, dedicated the Hendrickson House, and oversaw the firing of a cannon from the Swedish warship *Vasa* in Rodney Square. The cannon had been shipped from Sweden.

Presenting the plaque denoting Old Swedes Church a national historic landmark is Vice Pres. Lyndon B. Johnson. Landmark status was conferred in 1961. The model of the ship *Kalmar Nyckel*, which brought the small company of Swedes and Finns to establish the colony of New Sweden in 1638, is seen at right. The ceremony was held March 29, 1963.

For the American bicentennial, King Carl XVI Gustaf of Sweden made the first ever state visit to the United States by a reigning Swedish monarch in April 1976, marking a warming in Swedish-American relations after the Vietnam War. He planted a rhododendron at the northwest corner of Old Swedes Church, an homage to his grandfather King Gustaf VI Adolf, a rhododendron expert who created a world-famous garden at his summer residence, Sofiero Castle.

King Carl XVI Gustaf, crowned in 1973, has been a regular visitor to Old Swedes with Queen Silvia. In 1988, they embarked on a 17-city tour of the United States to celebrate the 350th anniversary of the founding of the colony of New Sweden. In Wilmington, the king and queen reenacted the landing of the Swedes, traveling in a 17th-century replica longboat up the Christina River to The Rocks. (Eric Crossan.)

In 2013, Delaware celebrated the 375th anniversary of its earliest permanent European settlement—the colony of New Sweden. "They came in search of trade 375 years ago," said King Carl XVI Gustaf of the early Swedes and Finns, adding that they also "planted a deep-rooted seed of friendship." The king and Queen Silvia were accompanied on this visit by the speaker of the parliament of Finland, Eero Heinäluoma. The first ships in 1638 carried both Swedes and Finns—Finland, at that time, was part of the Swedish empire. The royal party sailed up the Christina River on the replica *Kalmar Nyckel* to The Rocks and Fort Christina. From there, they came to Old Swedes for an evening service. Here, the rector of Trinity Episcopal Parish, Rev. Patricia S. Downing (left), welcomes Queen Silvia (center), Speaker Heinäluoma (behind the queen), and King Carl XVI Gustaf (right) to Old Swedes. (Trinity Episcopal Church.)

May 11, 2015, was a landmark day in Old Swedes history when, with the stroke of a pen, the church and burial ground were added to First State National Historical Park. The ceremony marked the culmination of a years-long campaign by Delaware senator Tom Carper to establish a national park in Delaware. Shown at the signing are, from left to right, Ethan McKinley, the park's first superintendent; Rev. Patricia Downing, rector; Right Rev. Wayne Wright, Episcopal bishop of Delaware; and Senator Carper. "It's incredible history," Carper remarked. "Old Swedes links Delaware to the earliest days of its existence as a colonial settlement," said Superintendent McKinley, "and Delaware's history echoes from every stone, grave marker and pew." First State National Historical Park includes five other sites in addition to Old Swedes: Fort Christina, the New Castle Court House Museum, the Dover Green, Brandywine Valley, and the John Dickinson Plantation.

Rectors of Holy Trinity

Rev. Magister Eric Björk, 1697–1714
Rev. Andrew Hesselius, 1714–1722
Rev. Magister Abraham Lidenius (assistant for about three years)
Rev. Magister Samuel Hesselius, 1722–1731
Rev. John Enneberg, 1731–1742
Rev. Magister Peter Tranberg, 1742–1748
Rev. Magister Israel Acrelius, 1749–1756
Rev. Magister Ericus Unander, 1756–1759
Rev. Magister Andrew Borrell, 1759–1768
Rev. Magister Lawrence Girelius, 1768–1791
Jurisdiction transferred to Protestant Episcopal Church in 1791
Rev. Joseph Clarkson, 1792–1799
Rev. William Pryce, 1800–1812
Rev. William Wickes, 1814–1817
Rev. Levi Bull, 1818–1819
Rev. Richard D. Hall, 1819–1822
Rev. Ralph Williston, 1822–1827
Rev. Pierce Connelly, 1827–1828
Trinity Chapel completed in 1830
Rev. Isaac Pardee, 1828–1835
Rev. Hiram Adams, 1835–1838
Rev. John Williamson McCullough, DD, 1838–1847
Rev. Edwin M. Van Deusen [Van Dusen], DD, 1848–1852
Rev. Charles Breck, DD, 1853–1870
Rev. William J. Frost, DD, 1871–1881
Second Trinity Chapel completed in 1881
Rev. Henry B. Martin, MD, DD, 1881–1886
Trinity Episcopal cornerstone laid in 1890; first service held in 1891
Rev. H. Ashton Henry, 1887–1904
Rev. Frederick Maurice Kirkus, DD, 1905–1930
Rev. Charles F. Penniman, 1930–1945
Rev. Donald Williamson Mayberry, 1946–1957
Rev. Percy F. Rex, 1957–1968
Rev. Robert MacLeod Smith, 1968–1986
Rev. Luis Leon, 1988–1994
Rev. Anne Berry Bonnyman, 1995–2006
Rev. Patricia S. Downing, 2008–present

TIMELINE

1697	Three Swedish missionaries arrive at Tranhook, including Rev. Erik Björk, first pastor of the congregation. Site and plans for new church chosen.
1698	May 28, the cornerstone of the present church building laid.
1699	June 4, Trinity Sunday, church consecrated.
1740	Two buttresses on north side of church added.
1760	South porch added to buttress the failing wall of the church.
1774	Gallery built to increase seating, accessed by exterior stairs.
1776–1777	British soldiers quartered in church.
1791	Last Swedish pastor departs; jurisdiction of church transferred to the Protestant Episcopal Church.
1803	Brick tower and wooden belfry added.
1830	Services discontinued; congregation moves to newly built Trinity Chapel.
1842	Church repaired and reopened for worship.
1847	First vicar installed; parish organization with two congregations worshiping in two churches established .
1847	Gothic Revival arched gateway constructed at northwest corner of churchyard.
1847	Northeast porch enclosed and made into sacristy.
1852	Additional heating stove and replacement bell purchased.
1882	Trinity congregation moves from Fifth and King Streets chapel to new church on Adams Street at Delaware Avenue.
1886	Memorial stained glass window (Breck) installed, followed by Forrest (1889), the sacristy and Bayard (1891), Millikin (1892), and Vandever (1897) windows.
1887	Parish house at Seventh and Church Streets built; enlarged in 1893.
1890	Cornerstone laid for present-day Trinity Episcopal Church.
1899	Comprehensive restoration of church for bicentennial, celebrated on Trinity Sunday, May 28.
1923	Boiler and radiators installed to provide central heating in the church.
1938	300th anniversary of New Sweden; ceremonies attended by Pres. Franklin D. Roosevelt and Crown Prince Bertil of Sweden.
1946–1947	Garden Club of Wilmington initiates a two-year project to restore churchyard.
1947	Holy Trinity (Old Swedes Church) Foundation incorporated to promote the history of the site and care for its buildings.
1948	Parish house renovated and enlarged to house the Christina Community Center.
1958	Hendrickson House donated by the Vertol Aircraft Co.
1961	Holy Trinity (Old Swedes) Church designated a registered national historic landmark.
1963	325th anniversary of the landing of Swedish colonists; Fort Christina State Park dedicated.
1964	Fire caused by a lightning strike destroys church roof and damages belfry.
1976	Community center playground replaced with plaza and amphitheater.
2003	Crown Princess Victoria of Sweden visits to celebrate 365th anniversary, plants rhododendron in churchyard.
2013	King Carl XVI Gustaf and Queen Silvia visit to celebrate 375th anniversary.
2015	Old Swedes Church and Burial Ground designated a unit of First State National Historical Park.

Discover Thousands of Local History Books Featuring Millions of Vintage Images

Arcadia Publishing, the leading local history publisher in the United States, is committed to making history accessible and meaningful through publishing books that celebrate and preserve the heritage of America's people and places.

Find more books like this at
www.arcadiapublishing.com

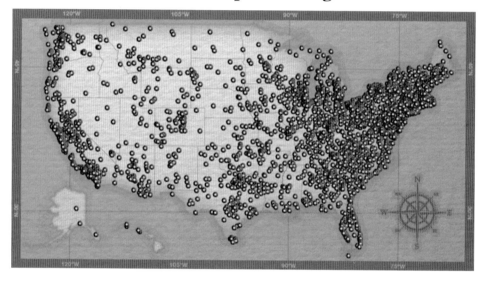

Search for your hometown history, your old stomping grounds, and even your favorite sports team.